HOW COULD GOD
LET THIS HAPPEN?

Campus Life Books

After You Graduate
Alive
The Campus Life Guide to Surviving High School
Do You Sometimes Feel Like a Nobody?
The Edge of Hell
The Lighter Side of Campus Life
A Love Story
Making Life Make Sense
Questions? Answers!
You Call This a Family?

HOW COULD GOD LET THIS HAPPEN?

JIM LONG

A DIVISION OF CTi
CampusLife
BOOKS

TYNDALE HOUSE
PUBLISHERS, INC.
WHEATON, ILLINOIS

All Bible quotations are taken from the New International Version © 1978 by New York International
Bible Society.

First printing, November 1986
Library of Congress Catalog Card Number 86-51135
ISBN 0-8423-1377-X
Copyright 1986 by Campus Life Books, a division of CTi
All rights reserved
Printed in the United States of America

Who shall separate us from the love of Christ? Shall trouble or hardship or persecution or famine or nakedness or danger or sword? As it is written: "For your sake we face death all day long; we are considered as sheep to be slaughtered." No, in all these things we are more than conquerors through him who loved us. For I am convinced that neither death nor life, neither angels nor demons, neither the present nor the future, nor any powers, neither height nor depth, nor anything else in all creation, will be able to separate us from the love of God that is in Christ Jesus our Lord.
Romans 8:35-39

CONTENTS

FIRST WORDS

This planet we all call home is bizarre. Planes crash. Tornadoes rearrange rural communities. Death claims newborn babies. It's a wonder anyone stumbles through life still believing in God.

How can a person maintain faith in the face of such tragedy?

And yet, for me, the question of maintaining faith was prompted by far less dramatic tragedies. I did not first question why God permitted the world's extreme suffering. I questioned why things weren't better *for me*. And my problems were not dramatic. I wanted to know why I had visual problems. Why things weren't smoother with my peers. Or my parents. I first struggled over my poor eyesight and my insecurities, and only as an afterthought asked God about someone else's paralysis. Or hunger. Or severe depression.

It's hard for me to own up to this, for I know it shows my self-ishness. But it also shows how personal our struggles with hardship and faith usually are. The question, "God, why me?" is not, it seems, reserved for the crippled. It is on the tips of all our tongues. We face failure, or sickness, or grief—even comparatively minor disappointment—and almost reflexively voice the question: *Why me? How could God let this happen?*

Hardship and faith meet. They clash. How can they coexist? How do we maintain faith in the face of tragedy?

Some people simply deny faith. *How can a loving God stand by, inactive?*

Others cannot embrace the pain of life without faith and so they deny tragedy—try to "faith it away." *If only I can believe hard enough, Grandma will be healed. Dad will find a job. I will find a wife. Judy will shake the flu.* And so they blink their eyes of faith at tragedy to make it vanish: *Abracadabra!* But most often their eyes snap back open to stare the same tragedy in the face. In this abnormal world, hardship is an inescapable reality.

I don't believe God swirls his finger in the sky to stir up tornadoes. He doesn't pucker his lips to blow jumbo jets out of the clouds. He doesn't grind cancer cells into your mother's bones, nor give you amnesia at test time. God hates pain and suffering, and ultimately will recreate the world so they will be wiped out of existence. But in the meantime, hardships—the mild, the tragic—do exist.

And so does God.

I believe in him. I perceive him to be good, loving, yes, even just. I do not see how anyone could stagger through life without him. But I am on a journey toward what I'll call Honest Faith. A faith that can survive a head-on encounter with hardship.

Consider this an invitation—an invitation to follow me on this journey. In these pages I have assembled a cast of friends and acquaintances who together present my mental journey toward Honest Faith.

Belief that tries to shoo away suffering by simply ignoring it is, it seems to me, Fantasy Faith. A mirage along the journey. I see these mirages, but I also see landmarks—definite, dependable insights that help put hardship into perspective. These Landmark Ideas are framed in the Bible and are clarified through our experience. As you read Scripture and reflect on your own experience, you will see many of these landmarks.

In this book I refer to seven biblical landmarks. Each one is stated and then illustrated by a dramatic, true story. After the story I use a few pages to offer my reflections before going on to the next landmark.

I am drawn to the image of landmarks because I do find the Bible's guidance somewhat sparse. It's not an open road we pull onto, rumbling past tragedy and toward God with our faith on cruise control. God has given us enough information to keep us headed toward him, but not so much that we race there without stumbling over questions. Instead, we meander from one well-spaced landmark to another, learning and growing as we slowly progress.

God seems to value our struggles, as if something happens through our struggling that does not happen any other way. Struggle forces us to put aside Fantasy Faith in preference for a faith that honestly faces the ugliness in the world.

And I sense God nudging me, as if to say, "Your faith will carry you! Step out on a journey to face life as it is. Until you can stare pain in the face and still believe in me, you will not truly believe in me at all."

FACING OUR LIMITATIONS
WHEN I AM WEAK, I AM STRONG.

"My grace is sufficient for you, for my power is made perfect in weakness." Therefore, I will boast all the more gladly about my weaknesses, so that Christ's power may rest on me. That is why, for Christ's sake, I delight in weaknesses, in insults, in hardships, in persecutions, in difficulties. For when I am weak, then I am strong.
2 Corinthians 12:9, 10

A FADING VISION

April of my senior year of high school. Smog hangs over the Los Angeles basin like brownish gray gauze. The air—dry, hot, and still—stifles me. And here we sit, eight high school friends, circled on the parched grass under the canopy of air pollution, talking. I look around at the lunch hour group, dipping hands into brown bags and whiling away this forty-five-minute break from studies with meandering conversation. Of the eight of us, three are totally blind and two or three are "legally blind" (corrected eyesight of 20/200 or worse). My vision, though poor, is good by comparison.

I observe, for the first time, that the blind kids all twist their heads the same way when they strain to hear, like Stevie Wonder. The others, the "legally blind," all seem to squint the same way, teeth partially exposed, thick glasses perched on the end of round noses.

It suddenly strikes me that I am associating with the school's "misfits." It makes me uneasy, as if their awkwardness is contagious and I might catch it. Or is it too late? Have I already caught it?

I see myself reflected in these friends, particularly in their attitudes and the way they cope—or fail to cope—with their handicaps. The misfit image haunts me.

How did I get matched with these people? Between second and third grade I was uprooted from one elementary school and bused five miles to another that had a resource center and special classes for the blind and partially sighted, along with its regular class schedule. To save money, the bus company had combined routes with those who went to the special classes for retarded kids that met at another school. Sharing bus transportation with those exceptionally troubled kids left an indelible impression on me. In my mind there were three kinds of kids: normal kids who walked to school, normal kids who rode big yellow buses, and abnormal kids—the retarded kids and the visually handicapped—who rode to school in *small* yellow buses.

Once enrolled in these special classes for the blind and partially sighted, I discovered that my first major task would be learning to type by the touch system on a typewriter with blank keys.

"Why blank keys?" I wanted to know.

"Just in case," the teacher responded.

"In case of what?"

"In case you lose your vision."

Other students listened to assigned reading on tape recorders or learned braille . . . just in case. This increased my apprehension and the feeling that I was "different."

My sighted classmates contributed to this impression, too. One afternoon I stood out in right field during a softball game. The other kids felt I could do the least damage there. I stood in that far corner, poised for action. I heard the crack of the bat and then, "Get the ball! Hey you! Get the ball!"

I was about to join in the chant when the ball struck my hand and careened into the grass. I was not the first kid to miss catching a ball, but in my mind that instant must have convinced the entire third-grade class that I was not normal; I could not see. From that afternoon on I hated P.E.

In junior high, years later, one coach ridiculed my lack of determination and told me of professional baseball greats who wore glasses. But the fact remained; I just could not see.

And, perhaps more than those earlier years, high school convinced me of my abnormality. I think of driver's training. Somehow I managed to get enrolled in the behind-the-wheel class. But I could sense my limitations as I drove the congested streets in a small white Rambler, plastered with "student driver" signs and jammed with students, each waiting a turn at the wheel.

Then there was my "panic stop." Out of the corner of my right eye I saw a rapidly approaching blue Plymouth. I'm sure that driver was bewildered as I slammed on the brakes and sent our Rambler rocking to a stop in the middle of that otherwise quiet residential area.

It did not surprise me the following month when I could not pass the eye test to get my license. I knew I could not see well enough to drive safely. But it did push my resentment deeper.

All of this and more formed the backdrop for my lunchtime introspection that hot afternoon of my senior year of high school. I concluded quite simply that I was a misfit—a terrible, hopeless conclusion. I realized even then that my poor eyesight wasn't the worst handicap a person might have—not like losing a leg, for instance, and not even like the blindness of my friends. But at that time, my visual limitation was overpowering to me. I had recently become a Christian; I had embraced the idea that God loved me. But I quietly questioned his wisdom. At times I even questioned his love, though I wanted badly to believe in it.

Why would he make me a misfit?

As I reconstruct things now, I find it difficult to sift out which of my hassles I'd blame on my visual limitations and which were simply a function of my age. In one sense it doesn't matter. The questions that I wrestled to the intellectual mat, pinned, released, and wrestled again were real questions for me. I assumed at the time that I was the only inhabitant on the planet with those precise problems. Absurd as it now seems to me, it only occasionally struck me that my brother or my sister or a "misfit" friend might be dueling with their own brood of ruthless doubts. Seeing life through another's eyes is an unselfish art to be cultivated; it's not part of the standard equipment we roll into life with.

A number of years later, after high school graduation, I renewed contact with one of those "misfits," my handicapped friend Bob Ayala. We met out in right field of the Anaheim Stadium in Orange County, California, at the close of a Billy Graham Crusade. I was counseling that night and Bob had come "to check things out." He had become a Christian a few weeks earlier through the influence of a blind Christian friend, another of the "misfits."

Through the years since then, Bob and I have had occasion to renew our friendship and to compare notes, to share our progress on this journey toward Honest Faith. Even back in high school as I struggled with my visual limitations, Bob was going through his own questions and emotional trauma. Hearing his story, as I have reflected on my own, has helped me put the question of handicaps into perspective.

Here is Bob's story.

High above California's everyday haze and life's ridiculously rapid pace lies the serenity of the Sierras. Determined mountain peaks poke their snowy fingers through the cloud cover and gargantuan redwoods rise from the mossy forest floor. There is a beauty, a tranquility, so intense you can feel it as well as see it. And time after time I have set my music aside and with my wife, Pamela, have driven the three hundred miles from our southern California home to Sequoia National Park.

Earlier today I gathered up my fishing gear and ventured down a rocky trail to the streamside. But as I walked, the end of the line worked free and began swinging and bouncing until (I later discovered) it was hopelessly tangled. Now I am perched on a rock and, my tackle box at my side, I begin the tedious process of untangling the nylon kinks. And for all the serenity that surrounds me, I am agitated. Call it a mood, or intense introspection, or brooding self-pity, whatever. But I am again confronted with my limitations and my frustration is intense. Clumsily I fumble with the delicate line, which I am unable even to see, and my irritation mounts.

I'd rather be deep-sea fishing. It is not so precise. The equipment is more substantial, the line a heavier gauge. I merely position myself by the railing of the boat and absorb the salt air and bracing spray. I am at home with the immensity of the sea—a broad, open expanse without the confines of rocks and trees and underbrush.

Confining. Far more than underbrush, my handicap is confining. Pam and I walked through an antique shop once, and that is precisely what I felt: confined. Uptight, with tension bordering on paranoia, I negotiated my bulk through the aisles. The room was an overpowering swirl of confusing blurriness. And my arm brushed a small figurine. There had been two: a Southern gentleman and a Southern belle. One slipped off the shelf and hit the floor with a mind-rocking explosion, spraying ceramic shrapnel across the aisle. *I* had shattered the antique. So we paid for a pair of figurines, but took home a lonely Southern belle.

One by one I have had to cross things off my activity list as my field of vision has narrowed and blurriness has claimed more visual territory. I should have expected it; my sight had gradually deteriorated over the years. But as a high school student something happened to change my expectations.

A blind friend invited me to go deep-sea fishing. One of his relatives had a boat and suggested he bring some of his friends along. It was my first time fishing and I was enthused. Several of us met at about nine the night before. We planned to get an early start and be on the water by daybreak. When I saw another blind friend, I commented, "Where's your pole? Don't you need some sort of equipment?"

"Don't need any," he said, grinning. "I'm a fisher of men."

I had thought the comment quite strange, but had no idea what he was referring to . . . until later. We sat up into the early morning hours talking about the change he had experienced in his life as a result of becoming a Christian. I had known Dave for years and couldn't argue; there had been a significant change. He had always been the jovial, rambunctious type. Now, as strange as it sounds, he seemed so innocent. The coarse edge was gone. He was still happy and outgoing, but he was *new*. Seeing Dave, listening to him, it seemed logical that I, too, should become a Christian.

The unexpected bonus came a year later when I returned to my eye specialist in L.A. I had such confidence in him. He was the first eye doctor to devise a pair of glasses enabling me to read. And I returned for frequent checkups throughout high school. Now he was telling me, "There has been no significant change in your eyesight. It seems your vision is, for now, somewhat stabilized." Something to that effect. But if he did interject a note of *guarded* optimism, I didn't hear the guarded part.

God may not have decided to heal me, I thought. *But he* has *stablized the problem.* The idea that he would permit my vision to deteriorate again or that the deterioration would accelerate was the furthest thing from my mind. Until one evening when I picked up a book.

The change had been so slow and unexpected that I hadn't

noticed it. Reading had, for some time, been an ordeal. The length of time between my labored reading sessions gradually increased. Finally, I had given up straining to read and just put the books aside altogether—until that evening. I pulled a book off the shelf, cracked it open, and discovered I could no longer read at all.

I could see the lines, even the words. I could discern that some words were longer than others. But the individual letters blurred together into an indistinguishable blob. I could not decipher them.

I used to paint. And although I was no Michelangelo, I enjoyed it. But now I could see only one small section of the canvas at a time, and even if I backed away I could not take in the whole picture. The detail work became impossible, so I set my painting aside. Several unfinished paintings sat in the garage—a reminder of my growing limitations.

Still my vision continued to narrow and my clumsiness increased. And with each discontinued activity, my questions grew. Why was God doing this to me? I had expected him to heal me, or at least stabilize my condition. But it seemed he was making things worse.

I turned to more physical activity, rising at 5:00 A.M. to run before there was any traffic on the streets. But if I looked ahead, I couldn't see what was right at my feet, and if I looked at my feet, I couldn't see what was coming right in front of me. So I alternated between running into tree limbs and tripping on holes until my ankles were weakened to the point that I had to quit running.

Aside from my guitar, singing, and songwriting, I found only one workable and enjoyable diversion: fishing. I'd go deep-sea fishing. Yet as much as I enjoyed it, I did terribly. Even when I managed to get a "prime location" in the back of the boat, it seemed that those in the front would be over a hole with excellent fishing while I caught nothing. And if saltwater fishing had its drawbacks, they seemed mild compared with the hassles of freshwater with its invisible line, delicate equipment, rocky terrain, trees, and underbrush.

All of these frustrations filled my mind as I struggled for forty-five minutes to untangle my fishing line amidst the beauty of the High Sierras.

The High Sierras. One of the most intense visual experiences of my life had been here. Several of us had jeeped into a remote spot high in the sequoias, and we stood looking out over the sweeping snowcapped mountain range. We were just above the cloud cover as the setting sun turned the snow into a blazing palette of orange, yellow, and pink. And as the sun dipped below the clouds, the light exploded. The experience was awesome. We couldn't speak. We just stood there, mesmerized by the splendor.

In all my life only one visual experience equaled that sunset, and that was the first time I saw the sun go down over the Pacific Ocean. As it did, it ignited a shimmering ripple that stretched for miles.

Those two visual experiences reminded me that there was beauty around me, even when I could not see it. And so did Pamela. Week after week I would pick up my guitar and form my thoughts into lyrics.

> *I have seen, I have seen the sun go down*
> *Behind the clouds*
> *   in the early evening sky*
> *And I have seen, I have seen*
> *   the rain of joy*
> *Fall from the clouds hidden in your eyes*
> *I don't believe that you could know*
> *   how I*
> *Appreciate the way*
> *   you've been my eyes*
> *And I have seen, I have seen*
> *   the water sparkle*
> *Amid the sun stretching out for miles*
> *And I have seen, I have seen nothing*
> *   that could compare with*
> *   one of your lovely smiles.*

Certainly with all my questions Pamela seemed to play a part in the answers. She had always been there. She had helped me sort out the questions. Even so, I struggled. It wasn't like I could once and for all settle the issue: "I am blind and must accept it." Instead, I repeatedly threshed through the same problem as my vision gradually left and I had to adjust to loss after loss. Yet Pamela had helped me see beyond those losses.

Pamela, there soon may come a day
When my colors will all turn and fade
But I know, but I know that
    that is when
Your love will shine for me
    to lighten up my way
Now I'm not saying I don't believe
    that he
Could work a miracle and make me see
But you know, but you know if God
    would give me just one more miracle
You know what I'd pray for?
I would pray, I would pray that God
    would give me
    a love as deep as yours.

And I had meant that. My character was more important than my physical inability. Far beyond my struggle to cope with loss of sight was my personal struggle with God. I tried to accept his resolution: He would use my limitation to build my character.

But have I accepted that? Or is that precisely what I am again trying to untangle as I fumble with my fishing line?

I undo the last knot and sort out my gear, then bait the hook. For the first time today I cast. Immediately I snag a branch and the line snaps. Another hook, more bait, and I cast again. But the stream is swift, the water tumbling over the rocky bottom. Again and again I try to drop my hook into one of the quiet pools behind a natural rock dam. But I can neither see the line nor can I quite "feel" it. I cast again, into a bush across the stream.

For a moment I stand on the bank and stare, disbelievingly, at the blur in front of me. Simultaneously something else happens; something deep inside of me breaks and the questions flood back full force. I feel powerless to stop them. God has taken away everything I have enjoyed, systematically, item by item—reading, painting, running. And what has he left me with? A broken fishing line.

Angry and incredibly upset, I return to our campsite, step into our small orange tent, and stretch across the ground crying. "Why, God? I can't enjoy reading. I can't follow the action of a football game. I can't drive, or paint, or run. How come the only thing I can do is play guitar?"

I feel like the world is closing in and that God couldn't care less.

"What's wrong?" Pam asks as she steps into the tent. She doesn't say much, but one thing she does say sets me off again. She mentions God and I bristle at the word.

"God doesn't care. God doesn't love me. Don't tell me about God. I don't want to hear about it."

She doesn't toss a sharp rebuke my way; she gives me the space I need. But her faith isn't shaken. "I don't know what the answer is," she says gently, "but I know God loves you." And she quietly slips away.

In my mind, I argue the point. "No, he doesn't love me. He doesn't care at all." And yet, even as I say that I know she is right. Neither of us understands it and probably never will, but yes, God does care.

And I can sense that this turmoil churning inside me is emotional. Somewhere in a deeper recess of my being I don't agree with my feelings and thoughts. Somehow, in some incomprehensible way, God is using this experience. It won't be wasted. Somewhere there is a seed for good. But my emotions are struggling to catch up, to match the stride of my convictions.

Two months later I decide to give it another whirl. I plunk down twenty dollars for a day of deep-sea fishing. And as is the usual practice, all I have to do is catch the fish. The crew hands will take them off my line, clean them, filet them, wrap them in plastic, and then drop them in my numbered burlap sack. When we return to port, I claim my bag of fish.

So I fish all day and really haul them in . . . both of them. There are no trees to snag my line, but my luck is pitiful. And though less intense, the same turmoil flares up again; the questions return.

At the end of the day, I go to claim my burlap bag and am shocked to find it full of fish. I lug it over to the crewman who cleans the fish and tell him, "There must be some mistake here." And I sheepishly confess that I caught only two legal fish. No, he explains, there's no mistake. An older gentleman, an *experienced* fisherman, had pulled in one fish after another. He enjoyed catching them, but not eating them. Aware that I was blind — and apparently lacking in skill, or luck, or whatever it takes — he had shifted his catch to my bag.

Perplexed, I mumble an awkward thanks and, with some effort, lift the bag. As I head for home, a strange feeling sweeps over me. I suppose I might feel resentment over the anonymous fisherman's paternalism. But that doesn't occur to me. Instead, it is as if God is saying, "Bob, you're not a good fisherman, but I love you. The reason you're not catching fish is not that I don't love you; you just need more experience. But here's some fish. Enjoy."

And though I fully expect a lot of unanswered questions are still ahead of me, I can't quite shake the quiet, almost irrational enthusiasm I feel, thanks to someone's anonymous generosity.

When I am weak, I am strong.

We could find far more debilitating handicaps than mine or Bob's. We could easily think of a quadriplegic, able to blink, to swallow, perhaps to nod, but nothing more. Or we could imagine someone who is blind, deaf, *and* dumb — a Helen Keller-type, trapped in a dark, silent, speechless world.

But the basic handicap question does not change substantively from person to person, handicap to handicap. Only in intensity. The doubts Bob may voice to God, prompted by his visual limitations, are molded from the same stuff as the Helen Keller doubts.

Contrast: An impeccable high school junior peers in her full-length mirror and frames an unuttered protest: *Why? Why am I so ugly?* And mentally we look on baffled. We brand the beauty a hopeless egotist, abnormally preoccupied with her physical appearance and its minute flaws.

Then we turn toward our own reflection. But imagine this: We see reflected not only our physique, but also our circumstances. We scan the horizons of *our* lives, pick out *our* defects, then whisper, *Why?*

I view my problems from within the chamber of my circumstances. And others view theirs from the insides of *their* circumstances. And we may all yield to the temptation of comparison: *Bob is worse off than I am, but my flawless friend has it made.* And the comparisons roll on and on . . . unproductively.

Thank you, God, that you didn't give me his problem! is not thanks at all. It's insult. Why not simply say, "God, you botched my life, but not nearly as badly as you botched his"?

To put it another way: We can brood over our limitations and tell ourselves that God isn't nice at all. Or we can face our handicaps with an eye toward eternity and the long-range values such a view sparks. We can walk into each day eager to learn what God is eager to teach. We can face each pain aware that our hurts hurt him too. We can confront each limitation knowing also that he has the skill to bring some good out of even the worst of circumstances.

I know what it is to feel weak. To sense my limitation. To know most clearly what I cannot do. I know what it means to wallow in self-pity, and then to feel guilty because of my self-centeredness. And then to feel guilty over my guilt.

I know what it is to feel guilty for thinking I have it rough only to see my minor inconveniences melt away before the true handicaps or hardships of others.

But I also know something of what it means to find God as a source of strength. I know, albeit faintly, the raw power of God that prompts reassessment of all that I consider weakness. I know what it means to find him to be enough.

The Apostle Paul had a problem that plagued him. It drove him to pray, "God, take it away!" And Paul learned that God doesn't always give what we ask for. The problem festered. The prayer went unanswered. Paul discovered that his weakness was to become the display case for God's great strength.

I think God still does that today: turns our weakness into his strength. Even the weak are powerful in God's strength.

I may still struggle with bitterness over my limitations.

I may still wonder why God does not achieve his ends some other less painful way.

But I have at least a clue that there is a reason for what he does. I have a landmark to give some sense of direction to my staggering faith.

And so I declare a truce with myself. I click some snapshots of my problems poised before this faith-clarifying landmark—*"When*

I am weak, I am strong!" And there, leaning against the wisdom of God, I rest. For the time being. Perhaps forever.

> *"My grace is sufficient for you, for my power is made perfect in weakness." Therefore, I will boast all the more gladly about my weaknesses, so that Christ's power may rest on me. That is why, for Christ's sake, I delight in weaknesses, in insults, in hardships, in persecutions, in difficulties. For when I am weak, then I am strong.*
> 2 Corinthians 12:9, 10

WHEN SICKNESS COMES
SUFFERING PRODUCES PERSEVERANCE.

We also rejoice in our sufferings, because we know that suffering produces perseverance; perseverance, character; and character, hope. And hope does not disappoint us, because God has poured out his love into our hearts by the Holy Spirit, whom he has given us.
Romans 5:3-5

SLOW-MOTION MIRACLE

Finding faith that can stand in the face of tragedy is a lifelong task. A journey. We do not arrive at such sturdy belief once and for all time. We are trapped in an abnormal world where hardship follows hardship, at times without relief. We may arrive at satisfying answers, but satisfying for how long?

Again and again our new experiences test our old conclusions. Again and again we find new ways to make sense out of suffering so that somehow, for one more day, we can cope.

Our own experiences raise or refocus the question. The experiences of others that we observe do too.

As a writer and editor, I often am confronted by the experiences of others. Several years ago I read with interest a letter from Dan Krainert, a student in California's Bay Area. Dan had suffered from such severe heart troubles that a transplant became his only option. He had a story to tell, he said. We talked, and it became apparent that he did. Not simply the dramatic story of his heart's failure, but the story of his struggle to relate hardship and faith; a story of facing the temporariness of life.

Monday, December 22, 1980. It was the color. In contrast to the sterile, institutional environment of Stanford Medical Center, the green foothills surrounding the bay bristled with life. Cars, houses, billboards, pedestrians, bridges—color animated everything. I was going home for Christmas.

Over the past year the hospital had almost become a second home. And as my heart condition deteriorated, it became clear that a transplant was my only option. But following tests six weeks earlier, further complications had set in. Clots had formed around my diseased heart. The pain had become excruciating. My heart had failed.

In response, Stanford moved me to the top of their priority list; I was scheduled to receive a new heart as soon as one was available. Until then, all I could do was wait for a donor, which meant waiting for someone to die—someone who had previously consented to be a donor, someone with the same blood and tissue types as mine.

The wait was traumatic. Although I was at the top of Stanford's list, it was far from certain I would be operated on. Many, I was aware, never make it to the operating table; they die waiting for a new heart.

My parents rented an apartment in Palo Alto so they could be near me through the frustration and loneliness of the ordeal. And my doctors, noting some slight improvement, permitted me to move into the apartment. As I waited for the heart, Stanford treated me as an out-patient.

I was on the transplant list for three weeks and nothing happened. Every morning I'd wake up thinking, *This could be the day.* But every day, nothing. Every time the phone rang I'd think, *The heart is in.* But it'd be a routine phone call.

And I would think, *Somebody out there is going to die. He doesn't know it yet, but one of these days will be the last day of his life, and then I will receive his heart and will still be walking around.* It was an eerie, unsettling thought.

As Christmas approached I longed for even a brief return to normal life—a break from the medical routine. Since for the time I appeared stabilized, the doctors agreed to let me spend Christmas at home. Mom and I climbed into our green Ford and started the two-hour drive. Dad was running some errands in Palo Alto and planned to return home to Napa later. After the confinement of the medical center and the tension of waiting, I felt liberated.

We cruised along California's Pacific Coast Highway northbound out of Palo Alto toward Napa. The radio was off and we hardly talked. Mom was battling the flu and the doctors had insisted I wear a surgical mask—not particularly conducive to conversation. Instead, I took in my surroundings visually.

We had no way of knowing that earlier that morning a nineteen-year-old Marine from Camp Pendleton, California, six hundred miles south of San Francisco, had been killed in a motorcycle accident; that arrangements had been made for him to donate his heart; that his blood and tissue matched mine.

Timing was critical. Doctors from Stanford would have to catch a private plane and check out the heart on location. If it appeared healthy, it would be packed in saline solution and, with the physicians, flown back to Stanford. At the precise time, the doctors would have to make an eight- to ten-inch incision in my chest—from just below my neck to just above my waist. They would have to saw through my breast bone, spread my ribs apart with metal clamps, attach a heart/lung machine, cut out my old heart, then attach his in its place. There was no time to wait; everything would have to progress with precision.

Stanford received the heart that morning, ran the necessary tests, and confirmed that the heart matched mine. At 1:00 P.M. they called our apartment in Palo Alto. No answer. We had left five minutes earlier. They called our home. My grandmother explained that we were on the road somewhere between the medical center and Napa. They called the radio stations to broadcast special announcements urging us to return to Palo Alto. We weren't listening. The California Highway Patrol issued an all-points bulletin. Still we cruised north.

When we pulled into the driveway at ten minutes before three, my grandmother rushed to the car to meet us. "Go back," she said. "They have your heart!"

"Oh great," I responded. "There goes Christmas."

Before we could pull out onto the street, the Highway Patrol arrived and the officers explained that I had to be back at the hospital by 4:30. With rush-hour traffic, there was no way we'd be able to make it by car. So with lights flashing, the Highway Patrol rushed my mom and me to the Napa County Airport where a pilot was already waiting.

We were airborne before it dawned on me that I had never flown before. And neither had my sick mother. The pilot reassuringly brushed aside our request for a bag (just in case) and then turned the flight into a scenic tour of San Francisco Bay.

When we landed, an ambulance was waiting on the runway. The attendants strapped me in and we took off, sirens blaring, for Stanford Medical Center. At 4:26, with only four minutes to spare, we burst through the emergency room doors. A man was pacing the floor. Had I not arrived by 4:30, he would have received the heart.

I was wheeled into a side room and prepped for surgery, then, around 7:00, rolled into the operating room. The deep green room was bright with light, music was playing, and a cordial doctor with a British accent stepped up and put a mask over my face.

"Oxygen," he said.

When things started going black, I knew he had lied.

My heart condition had been a long-standing problem. Shortly after my birth, July 3, 1962, my mom had noticed problems. Something was wrong, she was sure. I wasn't growing right. I wasn't taking nourishment properly. She expressed her concern to the pediatrician at my six-week checkup. He didn't say much, but referred us to a cardiologist in San Francisco. Through a cardiac catheterization he determined that I was suffering from a heart muscle disease called *fibroelastosis.* I also had mitral insufficiency—a leaky heart valve. With that disorder, instead of opening and closing normally, the mitral valve starts dripping. Mine ran like a faucet. The doctor didn't expect me to live past my first birthday. The condition could not be corrected surgically. As a last resort they put me on digitalis, a medication intended to increase the strength and effectiveness of the heart and to regulate my heartbeat.

The developments surprised them. I started growing right and eating as I should. I was, in fact, turning out to be a rather normal, active child, which caused the doctors to doubt their initial diagnosis. If I suffered from fibroelastosis, how could I have become so active?

They were sure I had the mitral insufficiency. But that posed only minor limitations. I couldn't run as fast or as far as the other kids. I tired more quickly and perspired more profusely. And I couldn't play contact sports, like wrestling. If I overexerted, I would pass out. But aside from these, the restrictions were minimal. We were also assured that if I was careful, the condition was not dangerous.

At age eleven, the doctors discontinued the digitalis. They wanted to see how things would develop without the added medication. And there was no significant change – until six years later in a high school drama class.

It affected my throat first – an odd pain that slowly began to spread. There was a sensation of tightness, as if I had swallowed something too large and it was wedged in my windpipe. My jaw tightened, my teeth clenched inadvertently. It was difficult to speak. The back of my neck tensed and pains shot down the underside of my arms and blazed across my chest. A crushing pressure settled over me. I couldn't sit down. As I stood, the pain lessened slightly. I tried to sit down again; the heaviness returned. My lungs felt squeezed together and I couldn't catch my breath. I stood up again, my face blanched.

"What's wrong?"

It was my drama teacher. He had been working with some classmates as they practiced their scenes. When the pain struck, he could read its intensity in my face.

"You gonna be OK?"

"I hope so. I really don't know what's happening." I forced out the words, almost breathlessly.

Drama class was really laid back. We met in a red-carpeted, high-ceilinged room behind the stage in the Little Theater. Chairs and desks were scattered to one side of the room with no particular order. Students who weren't rehearsing were free to sit around and talk. With that environment, it was less awkward to slip out of the room and walk next door to the cafeteria. Even as I walked crushing pains shot through me, though they were more intense when I stopped.

It was about 11:20 Monday morning and the cafeteria was already open. I picked up a milk and returned to class as the pains subsided. The whole ordeal was over in about five minutes. But it left me scared and confused. I didn't know what it was or if it would come back. But I *did* know it resembled all I'd heard about heart attacks.

I told my parents about the incident. They were not really alarmed. But they decided to take me to the doctor later in the week when he returned from his vacation.

The next day, Tuesday, at about the same time, it happened again. A friend was working on a project in a classroom and I was going to the cafeteria. "Can I get you anything?" I asked; then, noting his order, I left.

After I picked up the food and was returning to the room with the tray, the pain returned—the same stiffness, the same pressure. But I kept walking. As I stepped into the room, my friend immediately noticed something was wrong. I explained the pains and related what had happened the day before.

"Maybe you ought to be a little worried," he told me. Then, as the pains passed, we turned to other conversation. But that night I had the same difficulty and spent the whole night sitting up.

The following night, the pains again returned. The attacks came three times, one right after another. Five minutes of excruciating pain. A pause. Five minutes of pain. Pause. Pain. It left me with a heaviness that made it almost impossible to recline.

The next day I saw my doctor, the same doctor I had seen as an infant. He listened to my account without saying much, as he had listened quietly to my mom seventeen years earlier. And he called the same San Francisco cardiologist he had referred me to before. The cardiologist explained that I was suffering a heart failure, and he admitted me to the hospital at the University of California in San Francisco.

I didn't remember being hospitalized before. And as I sat in the corridor, waiting for a room, I was overcome with the busyness and confusion. I felt agitated and I wondered what this experience was going to be like. I stood up to walk around. The doctor insisted I be seated.

"You're sick," he told me. "You need to sit down." Then he added, "You're lucky you're still alive."

When he said that, the gravity of my situation settled over me. And I didn't know how to react. I didn't feel that sick.

The place swirled in commotion for the next two weeks. Doctors and nurses worked over me almost constantly, trying to pinpoint my problem. Again and again, I thought, *I've never received this much attention before. They must be serious about this.*

Finally, on a rainy day two weeks later, the doctors released me, confident they had found a combination of medications that would regulate my problem. It was good to be going home, my condition stabilized.

The rest of my junior year blurs into a haze. I was in and out of the hospital almost constantly. Between heart failures and hospitalizations, I somehow managed to attend classes enough to pass my junior year. But it was clear that my heart was deteriorating rapidly.

I developed atrial fibrillation—a condition in which my heart pounded erratically, faster and faster. This was dangerous because my heart just kept accelerating to twice the normal rate. If the heart beats too fast, that can be fatal. At one point the doctors were ready to attempt to stabilize my heart rate using electric paddles—a defibrillating device that administers an electric shock. They were finally able to regulate the problem with medication.

I developed an inflammation around the sac of the heart. It, too, was incredibly painful and seemed like it would never go away.

Each hospital stay lasted two or three weeks. And when I wasn't in the hospital, I was often home, too sick to attend classes. When I could go to class, I carried a stethoscope to monitor my heart rate.

The emerging problem was doubly discouraging, because it was obviously so complex. I had several different conditions, but they all amounted to one main problem: My heart was a mess.

Since one of my disorders affected my appetite, I began to lose weight. Things deteriorated quickly.

Halfway through my junior year, my cardiologist planted the idea to consider a heart transplant. His reasoning: "If you get to the point where you can't function, can't go to school, you might consider a transplant. Now's not the time. But if things get really bad, there is that one last resort."

As summer approached, I felt isolated from my friends. I wasn't getting better. I was taking more than twenty pills a day, but the medication didn't seem particularly effective. Incredible discouragement set in, and I remembered a simple phrase I had heard the previous summer, just before the heart problems developed: "Are you sure you have eternal life?"

I had been watching a Billy Graham Crusade on television one July night and his question arrested my attention. And I thought,

I'm not at all sure. I believed in God. But I had never really considered how that should affect the way I looked at life. As I fo-
cused on that TV sermon, I found myself getting excited as I
picked up a hint of how God wanted me to live.

Since Billy Graham preached from the Bible, I went and
bought a Bible the next day and started reading. Because I didn't
understand everything I read, I decided I needed to find a church
where I could get my questions answered. Suddenly, I realized I
was looking at life through changed eyes; I had a new perspective. Through my reading and my new friends at church, my
understanding of God grew quickly.

After the onslaught of heart disorders, with my life so ques-
tionable, my health so frail, that question I'd heard a year earlier
came to mind again: "Are you sure you have eternal life?" Death
seemed so much more real than it ever had, but now, at least, I
was sure of my answer to that question.

Fall 1980. In my mind, this was the test: *Could I handle my senior year?* By that time I had lost fifty pounds, was quite weak,
and continued to fight recurring chest pains.

Two weeks after school started I was walking to my car to return home and I just couldn't go on. The now familiar pains were
returning, but I was also overcome with weakness. I sat down on
the lawn in front of the school and told a friend, "I just can't
make it."

"What do you want me to do?" he asked.

"Go get somebody."

In a few minutes he returned with one of the school coun-
selors, who called an ambulance. I was rushed to the local hospital where doctors attached a heart monitor and took my history.
They didn't know what else to do and when they called my cardiologist he instructed them to send me home, that he'd see me in
the morning.

The next day I went to San Francisco. And we again discussed
the heart transplant option.

That night, alone in my room, I retraced the risks a transplant
would involve. I had paid close attention to the details. I had
talked to the doctors. I had read books and articles. I had seen an
NBC television special on the subject. And it didn't look too

promising. The statistics have since improved somewhat, but at that time, 70 percent lived one year. Less than half lived five years.

The surgery itself is a dangerous procedure, and afterward there are many other dangers to contend with.

I knew something of the side effects of the medication. Since your body identifies the new heart as foreign, it naturally tends to fight it. Powerful medications are given to counteract the rejection. Along with the desired results, the Prednisone steroids cause your body to swell. Your stomach, chin, and extremities bloat. Arms and legs bruise more easily. Bones become brittle and break more easily. Muscles deteriorate. Your immunity breaks down, making you more susceptible to infection.

A transplant was clearly a last resort. I would have to choose my risk: the risk of continuing to live with the danger of a poor heart, or the dangers brought on by the transplant itself.

The doctor had taken a neutral position. Frustratingly so. "It's something you do only if you have to. It's not something you look forward to. You have to decide for yourself if it's a risk you want to take. You can live with what you are, with what you have. Or you can take the chance."

I pressed him to express an opinion. Instead, he insisted, "It's not my decision to make. It's your life and you have to live with it. If you have a heart transplant, you're the one who has to endure it. I just can't make this decision."

But that evening in my room I thought, *I'm not getting any better, just sicker and sicker. I'm tired of being in the hospital, tired of wanting to do things and not being able to.*

By that time I had suffered from six heart failures and two cardiac arrests, all in the period of one year. What did I have to lose?

I slipped out of my room and walked to the kitchen. Dad sat at the dining room table doing bookwork. I pulled up a chair next to him and said, "Dad, I want to have a heart transplant."

He looked up, surprised by my straightforwardness. "Are you sure?"

"Yes, I am. I've been thinking about it and I want to go ahead with it."

He reminded me of what the doctors had said regarding the

risks. But he knew how much thought I already had given to it.

We knew, too, that Stanford received four hundred applications a year and accepted only forty, and that they administered a battery of medical and psychological tests. You have to be sick enough to need a transplant, but well enough to survive one. You have to have a reason and will to live. And you have to demonstrate the ability to pay for the preliminary costs of the complicated procedure.

Monday, November 3, 1980. After my second cardiac arrest, I was transferred from the University of California at San Francisco, where I was hospitalized, to Stanford Medical Center for evaluation. Medically there was no question. And meeting with the psychiatrist gave me opportunity to explain my Christian faith. That, after all, was my reason for living.

"That's good enough for me," he said as our conversation ended.

Then I waited.

Friday, November 7, 1980. Word came that I had been accepted. We still had the financial barrier, but were working on that. We went to the United Way and to the Heart Association, but discovered that they do not make funds available for transplants. My dad contacted the local papers, sharing my story and the financial need. My fellow students began raising funds. Our whole community got behind us. A trust fund was established, and soon $15,000 had been raised to cover the preliminary expenses. Things were progressing.

Another delay. During the tests, clots had formed between my heart and lungs. I would have to wait a month before I could be put on the waiting list. The clots had to dissolve first.

Saturday, November 15, 1980. I was released to return home and wait for the clots to dissolve.

Thursday, November 27, 1980. Thanksgiving. But the pain was so extreme I couldn't bear it any longer. I was admitted to the hospital in San Francisco. That night the doctors lost my pulse.

Monday, December 1, 1980. I suffered a cardiac arrest. The doctors had to use the electric paddles to restart my heart. That day I was transferred to Stanford Medical Center in Palo Alto and moved to the top of the priority list. But the doctors were not sure I would be able to make it until I got my heart.

Between December first and twenty-second, my condition improved some. The doctors gave me the go-ahead to spend Christmas at home. Then the heart càme—most unexpectedly, as they generally do.

The surgery, normally a four- to twelve-hour ordeal, went unusually quickly. My body was easy to get into, they said. After only two hours and twenty-seven minutes, the operation was complete.

I awoke the next morning with tubes in my nose and chest. Physically, my strongest sensation was the pain from the incision. But when my brother asked me how I felt, through the pain and the spacy sensation of the drugs I noticed something else. Before the operation, I had constantly gasped for each breath of air, as if a football player were standing on my chest. Now I was breathing without fighting for air. Before I had been conscious of my own heartbeat; I could always feel it, pounding erratically. Now, I couldn't feel my heart. And the one sensation I *did* feel— the pain from the incision—was a good pain. It was the pain that was going to give me complete healing.

The days that followed were laced with frustration, however. I experienced seizures, making it necessary for the doctors to put me on morphine and Valium. But beyond this was the isolation and loneliness I felt. Being two hours from Napa, I rarely saw my friends, and even when I had visitors they entered the intensive care unit shrouded with sterile hospital gowns and surgical masks—all I could see were their eyes. But considering the severity of my problem and the complexity of the surgical procedure, I did progress reasonably well. On Friday, January 16, 1981, after twenty-four days, I transferred out of intensive care.

Three weeks after the surgery the doctors performed a heart tissue biopsy. They did this by inserting a catheter with a clipper on the end of it through my jugular vein. With an X-ray fluoroscope I was able to watch the whole process. I could see my new heart pumping away. Then I saw the catheter snaking its way toward the heart. The tube's tiny jaws opened and clamped down on the heart, tugging at the organ. Then, with the tissue sample in its teeth, it retreated from the heart and out through the jugular vein.

Fascinating process. Depressing results. My body was rejecting the heart. The doctors increased my medication—more steroid suppressants to work on the adrenal system.

Hopefully the side effects would be held to a minimum, with no immunity problems, through the use of an experimental drug, Cyclosporin-A. (I was the first transplant recipient to receive it.) Doctors thought the new drug would yield a "better quality of life"—a positive way of saying *fewer* side effects.

By Monday, February 2, my body had pulled out of the rejection. I gradually improved until on Thursday, February 12, after fifty-two days in the hospital, I was released to go home.

Wednesday, February 18, 1981. My high school held a homecoming rally in my honor. The gym was packed and there were "welcome home" signs. The local TV station's mobile unit reported it all. But something was still wrong. Less than two weeks later, I was readmitted to Stanford with a heart infection.

Two days later the antibiotics took their toll: My kidneys failed. The high dosage of antibiotics made me sick and I started throwing up everything I ate. For the next five days, I felt rotten.

Monday, March 16, 1981. I returned home and began my personal rehabilitation program. This time there were no setbacks. By summer I was active again, swimming, running, bicycling, and playing slow-pitch softball. I was still taking more than thirty-seven pills a day, just to keep my system balanced. And the danger was not over; it never is. But I had experienced a slow-motion miracle and I was active again.

Tuesday, January 19, 1982. At one o'clock in the afternoon Mom, Dad, and I piled into the green Ford and headed south over familiar territory. I was due at Stanford by 3:00 P.M. It had been a year since the transplant and the doctors planned a three-day workup to check my progress.

I knew what that meant, and since the scheduling of the appointment I had been apprehensive. The heart biopsy was nothing too severe; I had undergone more than a dozen of those. What I dreaded was the angiogram, an excruciating three-hour test in which a catheter would be inserted through my groin into an artery, then moved up into the heart. The catheter would be changed twice during the procedure. A couple hours into the test the doctors would inject iodine, enabling them to observe the heart on an X-ray fluoroscope. When the iodine was injected, heat would flash through my body, igniting a burning sensation from my head to my feet. After the procedure, I would have to lie perfectly still for six hours.

Yet, even knowing what tests were ahead of me, I was optimistic. This necessary technicality, the test, would soon be over.

I checked in and met with the doctor who would administer the test, an Irishman with fiery red hair and beard. After preliminary blood work and X rays the first day, I made the rounds of some of the people I had met the year before. They were overwhelmed with my progress. One nurse who hadn't seen me since I was in ICU kept saying over and over, "You look really different, really good. I can't believe it. You actually had the heart transplant?"

I felt encouraged, reassured that this checkup would be routine. A simple test, following last year's surgical ordeal. Certainly much of the credit for my improvement rested with the Cyclosporin-A. It freed me from so many of the typical side effects.

Wednesday, January 20, 1982. I was scheduled to have the angiogram and cardiac biopsy in the afternoon. I was relieved when they came early. It would be so good to get everything over with and get back to my active schedule at home.

The next day I was greeted with the report that the angiogram was clear, everything looked great. I was free to go home.

"We don't have the results from the biopsy," the doctor told me. "That takes an extra day. But we don't expect any problems. We'll give you a call at home."

So I checked out at 11:00 A.M., enthused that things had gone so well. We were home by early afternoon. I was out mailing a letter when the phone call came, but I knew something was wrong when I walked in the front door and saw Mom's face. She had just hung up and had not fully absorbed the news. After a year of so much progress, after the encouraging results . . .

"Stanford just called," she began blankly. "You're in rejection."

"You're kidding."

"No, they just called. They wanted to talk with you."

I let her comment drift silently through the room, then pressed the question again.

"Are you *sure?*"

"That's what the biopsy said."

I paused again, considering the implications. "So what do I do now?" I asked, frustration coloring my voice. And she went on to explain the immediate changes in my prescription. Instead of relying on the experimental Cyclosporin-A, the doctors would turn to the medication they knew would work in battling the rejection, Prednisone. I was to increase my dosage from the token 10 milligrams a day I was taking to 100 milligrams a day, then return to Stanford in a week for another biopsy.

"Do you know what that will mean to me?" I said, mentally rehearsing the list of side effects: *brittle bones, weakness, deteriorating muscles, bruising, bloating, nervousness.* "I'm gonna look terrible and feel terrible. . . ."

I went to my room to be alone, as I had that night more than a year earlier when I had decided to go ahead with the transplant. And I began to question God.

I've been doing so well for so long. Why now? And I thought of a small group of Christians at my high school. They had been meeting outside the Little Theater each morning the past few weeks to pray for me, to pray that everything would turn out OK. But more than that, to pray that I would have courage and trust, that I would sense God in control.

I recalled a verse from the Bible, "And we know that in all things God works for the good of those who love him, who have been called according to his purpose" (Romans 8:28).

In all things . . . As I turned the verse over in my mind, I began to wonder what would happen if I could have a positive, trusting attitude through this rejection. Perhaps this trial, this difficulty would help me in some way. Perhaps it would help others.

That's when my focus began to change from the fact that I was in rejection to the idea that I could grow through this, another ordeal. Good could come out of it; my character could be refined. Suddenly it was as important to me to have a good attitude as it was that the rejection be dissolved.

Thursday, January 28, 1982. Again my parents and I returned to Stanford. My folks were concerned. The mood was heavier than on the previous week's trip. Still, though I felt a degree of anxiety, my spirits were good.

At the medical center, I was greeted by the same redheaded Irish physician. Thirty minutes later, the test was over and we headed for home.

The next day I returned from school and waited for the phone to ring. Nothing.

Finally, I picked up the phone and dialed Stanford. When I reached one of the transplant nurses and told her who I was, she said, "Oh, hi! How're you doing?"

"Well, I called to find out," I answered.

"Oh yeah, you're in rejection aren't you? Hold on, let me check."

After a pause, she was back on the line. "Dan, the rejection is dissolved. Lower your dosage of Prednisone 5 milligrams each day. We'll call you back on Monday and let you know what to do next."

I hung up, pleased at the results, but aware that I can never assume that I have arrived at risk-free health. But then, who can?

I remember leafing through my Bible. How forcefully the words hit me: "Now listen, you who say, 'Today or tomorrow we will go to this or that city, spend a year there, carry on business and make money.' Why, you do not even know what will happen tomorrow. What is your life? You are a mist that appears for a little while and then vanishes. Instead, you ought to say, 'If it is the Lord's will, we will live and do this or that' " (James 4:13-15).

And that was not written to people with diseased hearts.

Suffering produces perseverance.

Dan is convinced that his hardship has had some value to his faith. Let it be clear: God did not stretch out his hand into Dan's rib cage to squeeze the health out of his heart. But somehow,

Dan would say, God was around. His hand was in things, his fingers not pinching Dan's arteries, but shaping his character.

"Suffering produces perseverance; perseverance, character; and character, hope" (Romans 5:3). There is a purifying process set in motion by, of all the unlikely things, hardship.

But at such high cost, who wants perseverance? Who wants such costly character? We may protest, "God, couldn't you find a more comfortable, streamlined way to teach us your precious lessons?"

And yet, in Dan's experience, as in ours, it is not God who causes our calamities. We live in an abnormal world, still tasting the fruit of man's early rebellion. There is no escape from pain. Not yet. But the truly astounding thing is this: Once pain comes, God uses it to help us, as he used Dan's pain to help him.

The New Testament fascinates me on this point, for I find it an almost universal testimony that trials can be cause for joy. Paul says, "We also rejoice in our sufferings" (Romans 5:3). Peter discusses persecution and says, "Rejoice that you participate in the sufferings of Christ, so that you may be overjoyed when his glory is revealed" (1 Peter 4:13). James urges us, "Consider it pure joy, my brothers, whenever you face trials of many kinds, because you know that the testing of your faith develops perseverance. Perseverance must finish its work so that you may be mature and complete, not lacking anything" (James 1:2-4).

The reason for this, in each case, is that these trials, sufferings, or hardships set a process in motion that can perfect our faith. A partial answer to the question, "What is the relationship between hardship and faith?" is this: "Cause and effect."

Hardship tests faith, and in testing it, refines it. We can become stronger through trials.

To welcome the intrusion of hardship, to snuggle up to suffering and call it "friend," seems extreme. And yet I am reminded of the words of Peter: "All kinds of trials . . . have come so that your faith—of greater worth than gold, which perishes even though refined by fire—may be proved genuine and may result in praise, glory and honor when Jesus Christ is revealed" (1 Peter 1:6, 7).

Why test our faith?

Why refine it?

Why all the talk of perseverance? Of character? Of hope?

Because today's pain is not simply linked to improving our character *today*. Somehow, today's character development is tied to forever—to a future hope. So, for the Christian, no experience is wasted.

We each have only one lifetime to live. It may be littered with devastating tragedy. And yet, those very hardships polish our eternal character. They refine our faith so that today we make choices and value things that matter from God's perspective.

God allows our faith to be put to tragedy's test. And, if we can accept these hard words, even the most hellish of hardships can improve that precious commodity: our faith.

I do not write these words easily. I have been at the bedside of dying friends. I know how hollow "answers" can sound. And yet I grab hold of this landmark—*Suffering produces perseverance*—because it affirms that out of the darkest of circumstances, God can bring good.

> *We also rejoice in our sufferings, because we know that suffering produces perseverance; perseverance, character; and character, hope. And hope does not disappoint us, because God has poured out his love into our hearts by the Holy Spirit, whom he has given us.*
> Romans 5:3-5

CONFRONTING DEATH
OUTWARDLY WE ARE WASTING AWAY, YET INWARDLY WE ARE BEING RENEWED.

Though outwardly we are wasting away, yet inwardly we are being renewed day by day. For our light and momentary troubles are achieving for us an eternal glory that far outweighs them all. So we fix our eyes not on what is seen, but on what is unseen. For what is seen is temporary, but what is unseen is eternal.
2 Corinthians 4:16-18

A RUMOR OF ROGER

Dan's heart transplant story does have a dramatic flair: the lift that comes with, for now, a pleasant resolution. You might say Dan tiptoed up to death's door, rang death's doorbell, then ran around the corner without getting caught. Dan didn't die. At this writing he is still walking around, still telling friends and acquaintances — most anyone who will listen — that he's alive by the grace and help of God. And he's urging us all to live our moments as if they were gifts from God.

But the stories don't always have such exhilarating endings. Sometimes pain follows pain, ever deeper in intensity, and it all ends in a slow, excruciating death. Does Christianity have anything to say to one-way suffering and the death that follows?

I recall a story, written by Tim Stafford, about a guy named Roger. About his sickness and its impact on his school. Roger's school might be yours. And this true story, the one without the pleasant ending, could also be yours. Or mine.

The news came to Roger's high school the way news comes to all schools — in a rumor. It was winter: raw, wet, and cold. Kids getting off buses bringing them from Ohio farms clustered to hear the frightening words. Someone had heard that Roger was in the hospital, and that he had only a one-in-ten chance of living. The news spread quickly through little clots of people, down the old wooden hallways of the school.

Later a boy on the bus said that Roger would have a leg amputated, and some felt angry, some sick. Roger? Quiet, strong, well-liked Roger? Impossible. But the bleak March days wore on and Roger didn't return to school.

They wrote notes to him and sent small gifts they had made. Snow melted into cold, dripping rain. Basketball gave way to the first shivering track meets. For most, Roger became a shadowy figure only half-remembered — a body shrouded in the white sheets of a distant hospital.

For Roger the hospital became the real world. He awoke every day to the clean sterility of his room, ready to face doctors and humming test equipment. The warm, busy school was a hundred miles behind him, more and more a fantasy world.

His parents told him, after he had gone through days of testing, how serious it was. He had a malignant tumor on his hip. The doctors had originally planned to amputate his leg as high as they could. Then they found that the cancer had already spread into his lungs and chest, and amputation plans were called off. Instead they would fight the cancer with chemotherapy, as well as with cobalt treatments. Talking to Roger, the Sommers did not volunteer information on what his chances for life were, and Roger didn't ask. Perhaps he didn't want to know. "I'm not going to die," he laughed. "I don't feel that sick."

In any case, at first he didn't become the sad-faced ghost his friends imagined. He remained a farm boy, big for his years, and strong — an avid football fan, a lover of animals and the outdoors.

He enjoyed twitching a mouse on a string in front of the nurses, and he left plastic insects sitting under the Kleenex box. The nurses obligingly screamed for him. He had wheelchair races down the corridors of the hospital when he could, and he hung a basketball hoop on one wall of his room, so he could shoot from his bed.

The drugs, however, eventually had their effect. He vomited constantly and lost his appetite for food. Noise bothered him — he kept younger children out of his room. Movement became more painful. His body shrank.

Weeks later his lungs collapsed. A tube was inserted into his chest cavity to remove air escaping through lesions in his lungs.

For the next two months Roger lay in his bed, connected to life only by a variety of tubes. The open lesions in his chest refused to heal. His doctors had stopped the chemotherapy but continued heavy radiation treatment.

Eventually even the radiation had to be stopped, and Roger was moved to a hospital closer to his home. He was there for two weeks, and then, since Mrs. Sommers had experience as a practical nurse, he went home. Free from the tearing effect of the radiation treatment, he began to gain strength.

His chest lesions healed. He was able to move around once again. Soon he was walking on crutches, enjoying the warmer weather on the Sommers' farm. Had he been healed? Many of those praying for him believed that he had. There was, at any rate, a new feeling about Roger—hope.

Word of Roger's illness had spread, and in churches and small fellowship groups throughout the area people were praying with great confidence that he would be healed. The prayers encouraged the Sommers, but they also posed a serious question: Could they be sure that God wanted to heal Roger? Many of the family's friends thought they could be. They insisted the Sommers needed to pray with absolute confidence if they expected to see Roger healed.

It was a cruel dilemma for the family. "We wanted more than anybody for Roger to be healed," Mr. Sommers said, "and we knew that God could do it. We just didn't have the inner assurance that he would. It seemed like we had to be absolutely confident that Roger would be healed, or else he would die. We didn't have the assurance, and yet we wanted him to live."

In June, Jerry Burkholder, a dark, pleasant-looking young man, came to the Sommers' church as the youth pastor. He believed strongly in a loving, prayer-answering God, but he also believed in a God whose "ways are higher than our ways." He was bothered by the way people were praying for Roger, but kept quiet, unsure of the Sommers' feelings. Then he overheard a conversation that alerted him to the family's struggle.

"Roger had taken a turn for the worse—the lesions on his lungs had become more numerous and painful. There was a strong possibility of having to insert tubes once again into his chest cavity. In the middle of all this, I overheard a person—someone I knew was convinced God was healing Roger—ask the Sommers how Rog was getting along. The question put them under pressure. 'He's about the same,' they said. It wasn't true, and they obviously felt uncomfortable about saying it."

Jerry began to spend time talking to them about God's will, often in Roger's presence. "I wanted them to know that God could heal him, but that I didn't think anyone could know for sure whether he would. Wishing would not make it so. Regardless, they needed to peacefully accept God's will."

Summer came, hot and humid. Tomatoes and sweet corn began to pour out of the garden into the Sommers' house. The sighing of an occasional car on the road, the chirping of birds, and the distant roar of a tractor were the only sounds to bother Roger.

It was a summer of peace. Some days Roger felt good, and other days he didn't. On the good days he would sit in the sun on the porch, or he would go out to the barn with his pellet gun, hoping to get a pigeon. He liked to hobble a hundred yards down the lane to get the mail—a hard trip on crutches. On a few of his very best days he went fishing.

Few visitors came, and only Pastor Jerry came persistently. "Roger was a quiet person, not very outgoing," Jerry says. "I didn't try to push conversation on him, and I think he appreciated that. I would just talk to him about what was happening, trying to take notice of the things he had been doing.

"They'd made part of the living room into a room for him. It was bright and open—there were big double doors that were always open, and picture windows. It didn't seem like a death room, and Roger didn't seem like a boy who was going to die. It was too . . . too *ordinary.*"

Perhaps the hardest thing about being very, very sick is the loneliness. Friends are embarrassed. They hate to look at you, and they're afraid to talk about what is constantly on their minds: death and dying. The coldness of leaving all your past behind hurts terribly, and yet you're incapable of starting a new life.

You are weak, tired, and in pain . . . and yet your mind does not stop working. It goes over and over the past. You can't forget the drum of basketballs on the gym floor, the crush of bodies in the narrow corridors between class. You wonder what you would be doing in class—would you be in history right now?

Fall came, and Roger's friends went back to school. When he

had gained strength during the summer, many people in the Sommers' church and in prayer groups had taken it as a sign that he was recovering, and perhaps some had hoped he would return to school. But far away from the noisy, bustling first days of class, Roger quietly grew weaker and sicker.

"I tried not to cry in front of him," Mrs. Sommers says, "but he knew I did. My crying room was the bathroom, and he used to tease me about it. He liked to tease me, leave funny little notes for me in places where I would find them later on.

"He felt like crying himself, sometimes, and I encouraged him to go ahead. I told him the Lord understands how we feel."

Most days he lay on his bed, unable to move. Even with the numbing medicine he took, the pain was sometimes too much. Noise bothered him, and the Sommers wondered whether the forced silence was too hard on his brothers. They thought about taking Roger back to the hospital.

The tumor had grown to the size of a football on his hip—a hard inhuman growth that Mrs. Sommers sometimes touched when she gave him back rubs. He had three pillows that supported him in a certain position in bed, and they had to be perfectly adjusted or he couldn't rest. The work of caring for him, sleeping in the same room, praying for him, suffering with him became more and more taxing.

He slipped down. By late October he was barely able to raise his head to talk; his speech was soft and gaspy. The double doors to his room were closed. No visitors were allowed.

Friday was a quiet, dark day. Mrs. Sommers stayed with Roger constantly, leaving for only a few minutes at a time. His breathing was difficult.

At 7:00 that night Mrs. Sommers asked her husband to watch Roger while she rested. She felt exhausted, and slept soundly for an hour. Her husband woke her to tell her that Roger had said to get her. "He says he's going to die."

They sat with him, Mrs. Sommers holding his hand. Dan, eighteen, had gone on a date; Bill, sixteen, was out with some friends to toilet-paper a house. Tom, eight, had been put to bed. The house was quiet. Roger, who was very weak, labored at breathing. He talked a little. Earlier in the week he had said, "God could heal me like that *(snap)*—or he could take me to heaven." Now he talked about what heaven would be like. "I wish we could all go together," Roger said, "that's all. Otherwise, I don't mind dying.

"It'll be good to see Grandpa. We'll go fishing, and I bet we catch a million."

Dan came home, then Bill. Mrs. Sommers asked Bill about his practical joke, and he described it. Roger was interested. "Good job," he breathed.

It was late when the doctor came. "I don't think he'll last the night," he said. "You'd better get him to the hospital."

"But if he's going to die, why move him?"

The doctor gave him a shot of muscle relaxant. "Watch out, Doc," Roger said, "I've got tough skin."

"Call me if anything happens," the doctor said. He left.

The muscle relaxant had a quick effect. Roger had been straining on each breath. The relaxant made it easier, less painful for him. His breathing slowed, though he stayed conscious. Each time he let his breath out there would be a longer pause before the next one.

"You found yourself trying to breath for him," Mrs. Sommers says, "listening for the sound and trying to make him do it just by your will and your concentration. And then he would breathe again, and it would start all over."

His breath was shallow, barely audible. Finally, perhaps fifteen or twenty minutes after the doctor left, he failed to take another one. They waited for a few minutes, then checked his pulse. There was none. There were a few tears. "That's a relief," someone said, meaning that the long ordeal was over and that Roger could at last rest.

Dan went out of the room to look at the clock. The funeral director was called. The doctor came right away and after a bit the funeral director. Bill left the room and went to his own. When he came back down, Roger's body was gone.

Everyone remembers the funeral. Pastor Jerry preached the message in the Mennonite church the Sommers attend. School was dismissed for all who wanted to go, and Roger's friends jammed the front pews of the church. Some had come for the chance to get out of school, but others, close to Roger, had come with deeper motives.

Bruce sat with his head down so his dark eyes swept the church floor with secret anger. He'd heard the news on Saturday and had felt immediate anger—anger at God, or whatever or whoever had made this death. He'd been to the funeral parlor to see Roger's body and afterward he'd thrown up. When Pastor Jerry started his message by saying that this was a day of victory because Roger wasn't in the casket but in heaven, the anger flushed back in another wave. How could anyone call it a victory that a boy had suffered and died?

Duane hadn't felt shocked by the news that Roger had died because he had known it was coming, inevitably. He had come into the service and walked by Roger's casket, looked at his body, and thought, *It's the last time I'll ever see him.*

For Pastor Jerry the sermon was the summation of months of questions. God had taught him much about prayer and faith over the past months with Roger. Now there was an opportunity and challenge to use God's Word in answering questions remaining in many minds. What was the point of this ugly thing, death? Why did someone who was strong, good, well-liked, get wrenched out of the world down a painful six months and then into death?

He'd begun to think about the story of Lazarus' death, when Jesus delayed going to see his sick friend until after he was dead. Everyone—Lazarus' family, Jesus' disciples—had expected Jesus to go and heal him. Yet, John's Gospel says, "When [Jesus] heard that Lazarus was sick, he stayed where he was two more days" (11:6). Jesus explained, "Lazarus is dead, and for your sake I am glad I was not there, so that you may believe" (11:14, 15).

Some at the service had prayed with great conviction that Roger be healed. Why had God ignored their prayers? Others had come who felt, at best, bitterness toward God. They questioned: What kind of God did these people worship . . . one who killed teenagers?

John 11 put the question out in the open: Why would Jesus let someone he loves die? What did he gain through the death of a friend, when he could so easily have healed him? "Jesus said he was glad he wasn't there to heal Lazarus," Jerry said. "He allowed Lazarus to die, without interference, purposely. Do you know why?"

Then he began to explain that the service wasn't merely a time for sorrow, because Roger was in heaven, better off than he had ever been on earth. He would be having a great time there.

"And what about we who remain?" Jerry asked. "Jesus told his disciples Lazarus' death was really an expression of love toward them, the living. His death involved sorrow, and Jesus himself wept, but the joy of the occasion centered in what Christ wanted to teach about himself to the family, the disciples, and the funeral friends. The funeral was a greenhouse for spiritual growth. And not only that—many of the unbelieving friends who came to comfort got converted because of what happened.

"We have the same chance to see God working here. What about you? Where would you be if your body were in that casket?" Jerry asked, indicating the casket with Roger's body. "Would you be in heaven with Roger? Or would you be in hell?"

At the end of the sevice, he led a prayer of commitment to Jesus, and then asked those who had prayed it with him to raise their hands.

Hands went up—a lot of hands, perhaps twenty-five. And then the service was over.

What more is there to the story? When the days and weeks pile up, and the emotions surrounding the funeral die away, what's left behind but an empty space Roger once filled?

All through the Ohio countryside, in schools, on farms, in small-town cafés there are people who tell you that Roger left behind a great deal more than empty space.

"It shook up a lot of people here," Jerry says, "people who had been sure he would be healed if we had faith. Because if faith means believing that God is going to do something, then there was plenty of it. There were people who knew God was going to heal him. But, of course, God didn't.

"It's made me start studying the Bible all over again, to try to understand what those promises in regard to prayer mean. Like, 'And I will do whatever you ask in my name, so that the Son may bring glory to the Father. You may ask me for anything in my name, and I will do it' (John 14:13, 14), and passages like that. What do they mean? Could it be he was talking just to the disciples?

"I've grown a lot because of Roger's death, and I think those who were shaken by the fact that he died have had to restudy a lot of things. And they've grown."

For the Sommers, too, values have changed. There's less

fear of death, less interest in material things.

"The Bible means more to us," Mrs. Sommers says. "We read it before, yes. But it means more now. Now I can't seem to read it enough. There are so many promises."

Then there are Roger's friends who raised their hands at the funeral service. There are at least ten whose commitments have continued. They refer to the funeral as a beginning, a turning point in their lives. They met together not long ago, sitting around a table.

"I went into the funeral thinking, *I'll never see him again,*" Duane says. "I came out saying, 'No, that's wrong. I'll see him in heaven.' That made me happy for the first time since he died."

"I was angry that he had died," Bruce says, "angry at God."

"Are you angry now? Bitter?"

"No," he says. "I know he's in heaven."

"But why did it happen? Why do you think Roger had to die?"

They all look at each other a little as though they've got to find an answer for a lunatic.

"It was for us," several say at once.

"He died to bring us to Christ," Bruce explains. "I guess he was sorta like Jesus. He died so that we could know God."

Outwardly we are wasting away, yet inwardly we are being renewed.

What do we say to Roger as death approaches? Or to his parents and friends at his bedside, and then at his graveside? Our explanations are inadequate, our theories frail. Where does faith fit with life's dead end?

We might say that life is temporary. That we live in an abnormal world. That hardship perfects our character. That God walks with us through the darkest of times. That he has a place prepared in heaven for his own. And all this is true. Yet we flinch at every pain.

When death comes to someone we love, slowly, following a debilitating illness—as it did with Roger—it is easier to see death as *release.* When all hope of healing has been surrendered and we understand that separation is inevitable, we may find some comfort simply in the end to suffering that death brings. We may feel guilty saying it, but death may actually be welcome. The one we care about is finally free from pain.

But death does not always come slowly. A sudden, unexpected death—from heart failure or accident, for instance—robs us of the preparation for death that old age or terminal illness may bring. With unexpected death, grief is often more intense and prolonged. How can sudden loss be seen as a release from suffering and pain? Rather than suffering, the person who has died may have been at the height of good life.

In the past year and a half I have lost friends (and relatives) both ways—through slow, painful illness, and suddenly, without warning. As I write, these people and their friends and families are very much on my mind. I know, from my own experience and from theirs, how hollow words can be. Even with terminal illness, I am never fully prepared for the aching loss death is and brings.

And yet, less than a year ago, I stood at the deathbed of a friend, surrounded by family as death, "the enemy," came. But death was, surprisingly, at the same time, "friend." It brought an end to such prolonged and excruciating pain. All that long Sunday afternoon and evening, as my friend's pulse softened and her breath became more shallow, it was almost impossible to see death in any other term than longed-for release. That moment of death, far from being ghoulish or morbid, was instead . . . what? The right word, I think, is *holy.* That moment of release was holy. My friend was free. Outwardly she had wasted away to a lifeless shell to be ceremoniously disposed of. Inwardly, she was renewed utterly. She was free and now fully alive.

Can you understand what I mean if I say that I did not see myself as the free one because I was alive, but that I saw *her* as the free one because she was now released from this life and its sorrows? I am not "terminal," except in the sense that we are all "terminal," but somehow I was suddenly aware that I myself was bound—am bound—in my own slowly dying body. Even for the healthiest of us death is a release, a *doorway* to something better, prepared by God for we who know him.

We may not feel ready for it. We may fear it greatly. We may resent it as a rude intruder, the thief of our dreams and good times. But death for all Christians *is* the doorway to something better.

These thoughts filled me that Sunday afternoon in my friend's hospital room. These feelings lingered with me months later. I had come to see death simultaneously as worse than I had imagined—the finality of it!—and as not nearly so terrifying, not nearly so bad, as I had once felt.

But this is what has jarred me even more (and here I choose my words most carefully, for I find language to be so inadequate to fully frame my feelings): That friend's death has helped me accept other deaths. Not only hers. Not only mine. But as I have thought of death as release, and have thought of the need we *all* have to be released from this life, it has become easier to accept my other friend's sudden, unexpected death.

I did not feel the loss less acutely. And how can I estimate how devastated his family felt? But I was able to see his death also as release, a doorway to God's better life. This "release" felt hideously premature. We all struggled to accept the timing. Yet knowing that we—all of us, him included—are outwardly wasting away, made it possible to begin to accept his sudden death. Inwardly, he was already completely renewed, even before we (or he) may have felt his need of renewal.

There is another observation to be made, not about the release that comes after death, but about an inexplicable release that comes *before.*

I have seen it happen. Over and over again. Those most weak physically, find their faith soaring toward greater strength. I have visited those who have the least reason to feel strong, and yet their spirits are vital.

I think of one woman so weakened from battling bone cancer that she could barely lift her head off her pillow or her arm off the bed. But when I think of her, her physical weakness is not my strongest mental image. Instead, I picture her faint smile and a sparkle in her half-closed eyes as she used the last of her energy to express her faith in the goodness of God.

Outwardly, wasting away.

Inwardly, being renewed.

To be sure, there is a point at which the weakness of the outward body seems to impose its sluggishness on the inward spirit as well. Some diseases impair the mind and in the process appear to kill the spirit. People who are comatose do not recite Scripture, lift their hands in praise, preach glowing spiritual homilies. What's more, dead men don't speak.

Or do they?

Perhaps there is an eloquence we do not yet have ears to hear.

This much is clear: Christians who die do not enter heaven tongue-tied or glassy-eyed. They step into what is instantaneously familiar territory, and they greet by name an Old Friend they have never seen "in person" before. They are at home with Jesus. And inwardly they are unbelievably strong.

Between now and then, the processes of weakening body and strengthening spirit both continue.

Weakening body.

We may appear to be gaining in strength and beauty through the first third of life. But by the time we hit the halfway mark, we know we are weakening and death lies eventually, inevitably ahead.

Strengthening spirit.

But this very weakening of body contributes to the strengthening of spirit. It teaches us to shift our focus. To realign our priorities. To concentrate on things that always will matter, even beyond time.

Where does faith fit with life's dead end? This landmark gives a clue: *Outwardly we are wasting away, yet inwardly we are being renewed.* There is a greater life to which death is only the beginning.

> *Though outwardly we are wasting away, yet inwardly we are being renewed day by day. For our light and momentary troubles are achieving for us an eternal glory that far outweighs them all. So we fix our eyes not on what is seen, but on what is unseen. For what is seen is temporary, but what is unseen is eternal.*
> 2 Corinthians 4:16-18

LANDMARK FOUR

IN SUICIDE'S AFTERMATH WE COMFORT OTHERS WITH THE COMFORT WE HAVE RECEIVED FROM GOD.

The Father of compassion and the God of all comfort . . . comforts us in all our troubles, so that we can comfort those in any trouble with the comfort we ourselves have received from God. For just as the sufferings of Christ flow over into our lives, so also through Christ our comfort overflows. If we are distressed, it is for your comfort and salvation; if we are comforted, it is for your comfort, which produces in you patient endurance of the same sufferings we suffer.
2 Corinthians 1:3-7

A HURT TOO DEEP

Michael sat next to me in choir. It was a small church and a small ensemble. If we had twenty-two people at a rehearsal we felt like the Mormon Tabernacle Choir. With such a small group, and with practice week after week, we got to know each other fairly well. And even though I was one of only a couple high school students in the group, I became friends with the adults, particularly the other three tenors.

How can I describe Michael? He was pleasant. Mellow. Funny, but not hilarious. Clever, but not brilliant. Musically adequate, but no genius. He did not seem unduly depressed. Hardly the type to walk out to his garage with his rifle and take his life.

But he did.

And we were stunned. We who knew him, or thought we did.

Why did suicide seem so much less common then? Since then I have known several others who have killed themselves, or have tried to. One act of one person's will affects so many. The deceased is not the only victim. The forgotten suicide victims are those of us left behind. Those of us who must now struggle to relate our faith to this tragedy.

It is one thing to know that a brother or a father or a friend died of natural causes or of forces beyond their control. But how do you cope with the anger, the feeling of being cheated, when they take matters into their own hands? Such experiences leave scars that seem too deep to deal with.

Rick Christian tried to unravel the mystery of one suicide. What pushed Bobby over the brink? And how have his family and friends struggled to keep going in the midst of deep grief?

Headlights of a late-model sedan cut a swath of brightness in the black August night. Loose windshield wipers on the car beat a dull *rat-ta-tat* rhythm on the windshield, almost in time to the music from the radio.

At the wheel of the car, Bobby Benton tapped quietly on the chrome rim of the horn. He was happy and in love. The loneliness of the surrounding countryside—marked at thirty-mile intervals by all-night gas stations and populated by CB-talking truck drivers—could in no way temper his thoughts, which centered on his girlfriend, Joanne. She was resting her head in his lap.

Bobby and Joanne had been inseparable all through the past year. They had a lot to look forward to. Even though she was only a junior in high school, he liked to entertain the thought of marriage. They would have to wait a few years, he knew.

Bobby did not relish the thought of college, which could separate them. She would return to high school in a month, and begin workouts for the swim and track teams.

Bobby would try to get back to her as much as possible. He had told his former wrestling coach, Ben Parks, that he would be available to help train the younger athletes. Parks smiled at that—he knew the offer was motivated in part by Bobby's desire to be around Joanne.

"Sure, Bobby, we could use you," his coach had said. After all, Bobby had been team captain his senior year.

During the late summer lull that precedes the start of school, Bobby was working long hours at a car wash to earn money for college. After working two weeks straight without a break, he had decided to spend a few days with Joanne at the home of family friends.

They had planned the trip weeks in advance, and as soon as the last car had moved down the conveyor through sudsy water, great flopping sponges, rinse, hot wax, and the jet air stream, Bobby had jumped into his own car and, with a squeal of tires, headed for home. Joanne met him there.

"Look, I want you two to be careful. And Bobby, you drive

carefully," his mother had said as they were loading the car. He had heard the warning before—she told everybody to drive carefully, even their minister.

"He's got the good-student insurance discount; you don't need to worry," Joanne assured her with a smile. Before getting in the car, she turned to give his mother a hug. "Mrs. Benton, I've never told you this before, but I love you," she said quickly.

"Mom, we'll see you. Don't let Sis wear any of my clothes while I'm gone. She ruined my shirt last time," Bobby said as he eased the car into the street and turned on the headlights. He raced the engine loudly for fun and looked back with a smile as his mom jumped. "Hey, we'll see you," he shouted again, pulling away from the house. He honked the horn lightly as he rounded the corner.

As the car entered the stream of traffic, Joanne leaned across the seat and gave him a hug. She rested against his shoulder for a long moment, her eyes in a fixed gaze. Her fingers danced lightly through the dark curls of his hair.

After stopping briefly for dinner, they continued on their journey, which was scheduled to take them into the early morning hours. It was a gorgeous night for driving and being together.

"Say, there's the Little Dipper," Joanne said, pointing out the window.

"Nope, Little Dipper's over there, more to the right. That's Cassiopeia," Bobby said, glad to have remembered something from his Boy Scout years.

"You could have at least pretended I was right," she pouted.

As the highway stretched on mile after mile, traffic grew more sparse. Soon their only company on the road were the mammoth trucks, which, speeding by, delivered a windblast like the blow of a fist. Bobby gripped the wheel tightly and continued driving long into the night.

As the moon ascended to its peak in the warm, summer sky, Joanne laid her sweater in Bobby's lap as a pillow. "Sorry, Baby, but I'm sleepy," she said as she stretched across the front seat. "Wake me if you need help driving."

Looking down at her now as she lay stretched like a cat, he felt particularly close to her. Her elf-like nose, touched with a hint of freckles, was turned away from him, and he could see little more than her golden hair, which draped just below her shoulders. Though her skin was soft and tan, very tan, it glowed slightly green now from the dashboard lights.

Finding it hard to remain attentive once Joanne was asleep, Bobby turned on the radio for company. But the radio, despite the accompaniment of the windshield wipers and his own wheel-tapping, wasn't enough. Though he couldn't sing very well, he soon found himself singing softly to keep his brain alert. He serenaded Joanne as she slept:

> *Dear lady can you hear*
> *The wind blow?*
> *And did you know*
> *Your stairway lies on*
> *The whispering wind . . . ?*

But even that grew tiring after awhile, and he resorted to pinching himself to stay awake. It had been a long day. His eyelids seemed weighted. He thought of waking Joanne, but the thought slipped by. And then it was too late.

He closed his eyes and the car drifted off the highway into the gravel between the north- and south-bound lanes. The tires spun on loose rock, and Bobby jerked awake. Everything blurred. Grabbing the wheel, he cranked hard to the right. Joanne was awake and screaming—Bobby had not seen the massive eighteen-wheel truck beside him. Joanne's piercing cry was drowned by the sudden crash of metal on metal as the car careened off the rear of the monster rig.

High above the asphalt in the truck's steel-encased cab, the driver felt only a bump. Suspecting that one of his many tires had blown out, he looked into his sideview mirror. Seeing the lights of the car behind him as it rolled over and over, he pulled to the side and radioed for help.

It took workmen an hour and a half to torch their way through the mutilated frame to free Bobby, who was screaming hysterically: "Get Joanne out first. Forget about me." Though he sustained only minor injuries in the crash, he was too deep in shock to realize Joanne was dead. On impact, her body had been pinned against his own, and workmen found him holding her in a tight embrace.

A week after Joanne's death, all of Bobby's physical wounds

had disappeared. Yet, just how deep the painful roots of his loss reached, no one could say.

"I can't live with this, I want to die," he kept repeating to anybody who would listen. When he saw that nobody really understood what he was saying—that he actually *did* want to die—he retreated to his room, crowded with dusty wrestling trophies, dog-eared snapshots of him and Joanne, and assorted high school memorabilia, where he would cry for hours.

"We knew Bobby was hurting desperately, but we never knew how desperately," said his mother. "I just wish I could have taken the pain from him, or helped him carry the burden like I did when he was a child with a bad splinter or skinned knee. But we thought the grief he felt was natural—that it would eventually work its way out."

A young Christian with a developing, often wavering faith in God, Bobby did not immediately turn to the Lord for help. He felt the world he knew was crumbling because of his own stupidity.

"I took a human life and you don't know what that means," he told his family and friends. "I lost the thing I loved most in life and it was my fault," he often repeated, his brown, tired eyes brimming with tears.

For a time, Bobby's depression seemed to lift. He began to eat a little better and sleep more. He stopped talking about his desire to die, and started smiling more. He took a trip with friends to Lake Tahoe, and returned looking rested. He also asked to speak with the youth pastor of his church.

The church leader came over and the two went into a back room and talked. They spent long periods in prayer, with Bobby confessing to God his hurts, anguish, and fears. Most of all, he asked the Lord to remove the deep sense of guilt he felt over Joanne's death.

He came away feeling refreshed and forgiven, like God had given him a reason to continue living. And as he began to do more with his old friends again—friends with whom he and Joanne used to party regularly—his focus of concern shifted from himself to them.

He faced a problem, though. His faith in God had always been kept fairly quiet before, and only a handful of people actually

knew he was a Christian at all. But now he wanted to change
that. He wanted to share with his old friends how he had found a
new sense of direction. How God had forgiven him for his part
in Joanne's death and had given him a peace inside which he
hadn't found in marijuana, alcohol, or anything else.

One late-summer night he showed up unexpectedly at a party.
His friends seemed glad to see him again. Some of them had not
seen him since graduation the previous June.

"Hey, there's Bobby," came a voice from a darkened corner
near a throbbing stereo speaker.

"Yeah, here's Bobby," Bobby said as he stepped into the smoke-
filled room. "How are you all doing, anyway?" he asked to
nobody in particular, getting a response of assorted nodding
heads and half smiles.

They wanted to find out how Bobby was and what he had been
doing. He soon found himself in the corner, surrounded by a few
of those who were most familiar to him. He tried to keep things
light at first, but he was pressed with questions.

"Things are changing," he began. A few minutes later he said
something about Jesus. That name alone made people a bit uncomfortable. It was not what they normally talked about at par-
ties. He used the name again, trying to explain how he had found
new hope.

"Hold on," came a voice from the group. "Look, this is fine for
you. You can be a Jesus freak. But don't expect it from everybody, and especially don't expect it from me. Bobby, you can't
hedge the pain and memories with talk of religion."

"But it's not religion, it's . . ." His voice trailed off and he
never finished the sentence. He mumbled something about having to get home, pushed his way past the bodies, and walked
hastily out of the door without looking back.

After facing rejection from those he was trying to help, Bobby
returned home and cried all night. The incident festered inside
him, and he was never again able to step outside the depression
that once more engulfed him.

Bobby gradually closed himself off from those around him. It
was as if he stood in an open field at the start of a snow. Little
snowflakes began to cover him up. Slowly his image and shape
were covered over and rounded off until it was hard to tell that
the one standing there was the same Bobby.

Those around him all seemed to sense what was happening, but felt inadequate to do anything for him. Many talked among themselves about their fears for his life, but they had no idea how to respond.

"I was afraid to ask him how he was feeling at the time, even though I knew, because we had never before talked about deep stuff," said one friend, a Christian who grew up with Bobby and wrestled on the same high school team. "We seldom talked about anything more than classes, or what either of us saw over the weekend at the movies."

Bobby's father, a police sergeant, said he never confronted his son directly about his concern for his life because suicide seemed so out of keeping with Bobby's nature. "I didn't want to be the one to put the idea in his head if he wasn't thinking about it," he said. "Suicide was something that only happened to the other guy, to problem kids. I thought of it as something you read about in newspapers. It never actually happens in real life to good families . . . to your own family." But just to be sure, Mr. Benton kept his service revolver locked in a safe at home whenever he was not wearing it.

Others said they found it hard to face Bobby with their suspicions because "I felt he needed time to be alone," or "I felt he'd get over it and wanted to keep nasty memories from his mind," or finally, "What could I have ever said? I'd never experienced anything like he had, nor had I ever suffered."

Perhaps there was a time when somebody could have intervened to help guide Bobby away from his despair. But after a certain point, he made up his mind. He was going to die.

One day, Bobby took a walk around his old high school campus. While there, he spotted his coach across the football field and walked over to sit beside him along the sideline.

"Bobby didn't want to talk then. He just wanted a friend to be near him," his coach said later. They sat together for a long time beneath the bright sun, neither of them saying a word. Finally Bobby got up and quietly walked away.

He bought a picture album and began laying out all the snapshots he had of Joanne. He included pictures of her at the beach, at school, on dates, in her home. He included a fortune cookie message from one of their dinners out: "Your sweetheart or helpmate is true and sincerely devoted." He also clipped the lyrics of a Dan Fogelberg song. Entitled "Part of the Plan," the song begins:

I have these moments
All steady and strong
I'm feeling so holy and humble
The next thing I know
I'm all worried and weak
And I feel myself
Starting to crumble.

He worked on the photo album long into the night. He also wrote good-bye letters to his special friends, his parents, and Joanne's parents, explaining to them what he felt he had to do. The next morning he borrowed money from his dad for stamps to mail all the letters. By the time they arrived at their destinations the next day, Bobby planned to be dead.

After his parents both left for work he began calling friends to whom he had not sent letters to tell them good-bye; that he would not be speaking to them again. Most thought he was merely going to run away and tried to dissuade him from such a move.

Later in the day, he stopped by the home of a casual acquaintance and asked to borrow a rifle, explaining that he was going on a hunting trip. His friend took a single .22 caliber shell and demonstrated loading the firearm for him. Bobby thanked him and departed.

When he arrived at his empty home, Bobby made one last phone call to a girl who had been a close friend of Joanne's. His message: "When I hang up the phone, call the police and send them over to the house." She screamed hysterically when she heard the click of his receiver.

After hanging up, Bobby walked into the back bedroom with the loaded gun and placed it to his head.

His body was found within minutes by his mother who happened to get off work early that day. Police were seconds behind. In his bedroom, a sealed note to his parents was discovered:

"Ask Joanne's parents to bury me near Joanne. I don't think they'll mind," he wrote. Bobby's and Joanne's parents both complied. A dozen miles south of San Francisco on a grassy knoll, the two high school sweethearts were laid to rest together.

Bobby's funeral service was held two years ago. Although the interval of time has helped to ease the trauma felt by those who knew Bobby best, the memories cannot be erased, for his friendships ran deep.

"Bobby was just like a son to me: an all-out guy who led by his actions," said his coach, noting how Bobby would run twenty laps during wrestling workouts if told to run ten, or would do a hundred push-ups if told to do fifty. "It was the same with his Christianity. He showed his love and brotherhood not by just talking but by getting close to people and showing that he cared. I'm just sad that in the end he chose to go the wrong direction."

The struggles were the hardest for his parents. Their prayers seemed choked. It was all they could do to pray simply: "God, we miss Bobby so badly. Just help us make it through today."

They prayed that way every day, knowing God would understand the pain they felt. It was not so much the grandiose moments they missed, like when Bobby won a big wrestling meet; but rather the quiet, everyday moments like when he returned home from school and asked, "What's for dinner, Mom?" Invariably he'd lift the cover off a pot and ruin the rice.

But the greatest agony lay in the knowledge that they never talked to their son about their fears for his life. They heard his tormented cries that he no longer wanted to live, but they never really understood what those words meant.

"If we had confronted him, asked him if he was considering suicide, and then talked it out with him, I believe he would be alive today," said his mother, who now works as a volunteer at a suicide prevention center near their home.

Said his father: "I never once imagined this could happen in our family, and never talked to him about it. He had been such a winner before. But suddenly it was not just somebody else's suicide I was reading about. It was somebody I talked with and loved. It was Bobby. I just wish I had known. . . ."

We comfort others with the comfort we have received from God.

Where was the comfort for Bobby? His deep depression speaks from this story like a voice from the bottom of a well. Suicide is always that way. It forces friends, family, even the most casual acquaintance to ask, Where was the comfort? Surely death was not the only way out.

Yet there is no answer from Bobby. He is gone.

Bobby's story is an important reminder that hurt and doubt and depression can build to the absolute breaking point. That is when others must intervene, to absorb a small share of the pain, to think clearly for the person whose mind is blurred by grief.

No one did that for Bobby, and he did not encourage them to. Instead he took his life, and in doing so spread his own anger and grief to others. Bobby is gone. But he left his grief behind.

Was there no comfort for Bobby? Bobby thought not. But others in his life — his parents, for instance — would say that there could have been, if only. If only they had talked to him directly about suicide. If only they could have stopped him from taking that horribly irreversible step. If only they could have convinced him to give comfort more time . . . to hold on, even in his grief, and cling to the hope that God would bring a brighter day.

So the Bentons, whose son found no comfort, have dedicated themselves to seeing that others don't duplicate Bobby's — and their — mistake. They believe that comfort can be given even to those whose pain would lead them to suicide — if only someone is awake enough to offer that comfort. (And if the person considering suicide will receive it.)

We need to be aware of those around us. The Bentons would tell us that we must cultivate the art of listening. *Listening.* Only by listening can we understand enough of another's troubles to offer genuine comfort.

Where is the comfort? Bobby's parents can tell us, for they themselves found it. Their pain — the pain of any parent under such circumstances — was unimaginable. The awful pain of losing the son they loved more than life; the sickening guilt of thinking they might have saved him . . . can any pain — even Bobby's — be worse than what they felt? Yet they hung on, and gradually they found comfort. From God. From friends. And with that comfort they have been able to comfort others.

They did not discover it overnight. At first their emotions were so overwrought, their prayers so choked, that all they could manage was a weak plea for God to help them survive the day. They hung on, though, until comfort came.

And such comfort does not wipe away the pain. Pain like this marks us permanently. It may lose its intensity, but we don't forget it.

We carry with us an awareness of death that alters our perception of life. We are not perpetually morose, but we may be less tolerant of unending triviality. When someone suggests that God will shelter really godly people from hardship, we know better.

But we carry something else with us, too. We carry the discovery that we can find comfort even in the midst of the most perplexing of circumstances. The discovery of a sense of comfort so alien to our experience that it is almost as perplexing as the hardship itself.

Comfort from God himself.

It comes in many forms, this comfort from God. Those who have suffered most often speak of a sense of God's presence, the strong suspicion—no, *conviction*—that they are not alone. God is with them, walking with them, feeling what they feel, somehow communicating his care mysteriously, directly to their spirit. They speak of the comfort of prayer: simply talking to God honestly, in straightforward language, and sensing that he listens.

That same comforting God is eager to carry each of us.

Many who suffer speak of finding him and his comfort in the Bible, his Word in print. As we read, we relearn his strong commitment to us, and gain deeper conviction that he, the suffering God, understands. He knows pain. He knows the spiritual distress of facing temptation. When we who suffer read God's Word, we find comfort and the encouragement to endure. We find in the Bible a God who acknowledges suffering, feels it, and ultimately will obliterate it. We find a God who loves us and forgives us for all our shortcomings.

When we suffer, we also find comfort through others who have suffered—particularly, though not exclusively, from other Christians. Well-meaning, would-be comforters may stammer or blunder their way through some "encouraging words." But those who have suffered know what real comfort is. They comfort us out of the overflow of comfort they have received from God. Perhaps they have the wisdom to know when merely *listening* is enough.

As they are with us, listening, comforting, what was unbearable may become tolerable. In time we may find ourselves capable of comforting others as well. Others may meet us and feel somehow uniquely understood by us.

Life goes on.

And now, somehow, we know we can face it.

What of Bobby and others who have surrendered to their depression? Their choice of death testifies just the opposite of what we have said. They found no comfort. So what can we say about Bobby?

We can say very little. Words fail. We hurt with those who suffer in suicide's aftermath. And we cling to the hope that Bobby and others like him are in the hands of a loving God, who feels our pain and understands the desperation it can bring.

We cling, too, to our faith in God and his promises. God *does* comfort. He offers his comfort to all so that they, in their turn, can comfort others. Don't let Bobby, or any other, take away this faith in God. Instead let Bobby remind us that the God of comfort wants to use us as his comforters to people who, like Bobby, have almost lost the ability to hope for themselves.

The Father of compassion and the God of all comfort . . . comforts us in all our troubles, so that we can comfort those in any trouble with the comfort we ourselves have received from God. For just as the sufferings of Christ flow over into our lives, so also through Christ our comfort overflows. If we are distressed, it is for your comfort and salvation; if we are comforted, it is for your comfort, which produces in you patient endurance of the same sufferings we suffer.
2 Corinthians 1:3-7

HELP IN THE MIDST OF VIOLENCE
IN MY DISTRESS I CALLED TO THE LORD.

The cords of death entangled me; the torrents of destruction overwhelmed me. The cords of the grave coiled around me; the snares of death confronted me. In my distress I called to the Lord; I cried to my God for help. From his temple he heard my voice; my cry came before him, into his ears.

He reached down from on high and took hold of me; he drew me out of deep waters.
Psalm 18:4-6, 16

ATTACKED!

I remember most my anger. A friend's daughter had been attacked, brutally assaulted. I remember lying awake at night until suddenly I could not hold back a rush of bitter feelings, emotions as deep as any I have ever felt. I cried and clenched my teeth until my jaw ached and I forced out the words, "God, it's just not right." At that point, that odd prayer was all I could manage.

The emotion came over me and receded with minutes, but left me physically exhausted.

Some Christians would have me moderate my feelings. "Hate sin, but love the sinner," they would say. But at times I feel incapable of separating the person from his action. If I could call down fire to incinerate the oppressor, I probably would.

What am I left with? Bitterness that would incinerate me?

Bitterness is one possibility. But prayer is a better one.

I am amazed by prayer. Even a simple sentence—an honest question, a call for help—instantly puts me in touch with God. Moments before I may have questioned whether there was a God anywhere in the universe. Then prayer asserts plainly: He is at my side. Prayer reminds me that he is close and caring, even when he does not intervene.

In the story that follows, we get some insight into how one victim felt. Writer Steve Lawhead, who interviewed Stu after he was attacked, captures the emotion of the ordeal, but also chronicles the support of Stu's faith in the face of his tragedy.

A light dusting of snow drifted down from a swollen, overcast sky as Stu Caddell loaded the last of his luggage into the back of his Toyota Landcruiser. He checked his skis and poles atop the roof one last time and slid behind the wheel. Glancing at his watch as he headed onto the interstate highway, Stu regretted his late start. It would be after midnight when he reached Denver, where he'd join his parents for a holiday ski weekend.

It was already late afternoon of New Year's Eve as he passed the first interchanges. Few cars were on the road. Stu sighed. His family would be sitting down to dinner soon—warm and safe. A highway was a lonely place when there was somewhere else you wanted to be. But what could he have done? He'd had to work—boss's orders. *So stop moaning and make the best of it,* he told himself, then settled in for the long drive.

The miles and hours receded slowly as evening came on and the gray clouds changed to violet. Stu rubbed the heel of his hand across tired eyes. He was beginning to get drowsy. Fatigue was only natural after a long day's work, but dangerous when alone on the highway. "Wake up!" he said aloud. "There's still a long way to go." He cracked open a window to let in some fresh air and felt a little better momentarily. He shut the window again when it became too cold; soon he was feeling sleepy again. *I need someone to talk to,* he thought.

Stu had often picked up hitchhikers when traveling. He found them interesting, and once in awhile he got a chance to talk about himself and his faith in God, to share something he felt was important. More often than not, it generated some stimulating conversations. With that in mind, Stu began to watch for any lonely figures with a thumb extended.

The Landcruiser entered another interchange. High above in the icy air the huge sodium vapor lamps began to flicker. And then Stu saw him, a dark shape rooted beside the highway, solitary in the dancing light. The hitchhiker was bareheaded, his hands were thrust deep into the pockets of his combat coat. He wore army fatigues and boots. Stu flipped a blinker on and pulled the Toyota to a halt on the wide shoulder. The hitchhiker moved slowly, stiffly, as if frozen from waiting so long.

Stu jerked open the side door. "Hi, I'm Stu, where are you going?" He looked at the hitchhiker, expecting a reply.

"Uh . . . Denver. I'm going to Denver, man," he said. The

drab green combat jacket bore a name, Grimes, and some insig-
nias. The cuffs were frayed and the fatigue pants were stained.
His dirty blond hair was long and tangled. Stu felt a momentary
twinge of fear—if the guy was a serviceman, it had been some
time since he'd seen active duty. But maybe he was just down on
his luck and needed a friend.

"You Grimes?" he asked, indicating the patch.

"Yeah," the hitchhiker grunted. "That's me."

"You in the army?" Stu tried to get the conversation rolling.
That had been the point after all—companionship to keep him
from falling asleep. The hitchhiker seemed content to warm up
and wrap himself in his own thoughts. Stu let the question hang
as he downshifted and swung back onto the interstate.

"Marines," the man said at length. "I was in the marines.
Vietnam."

"See any action?" Stu watched the smooth, snaking tire tracks
slide away in the rearview mirror. The snow was just a light dust
on the road. No answer. He glanced at his passenger, noting the
listless eyes and the dead, unexpressive face. . . . He felt again
that warning twinge, but forced it out of his mind with another
question. "Do you live in Denver?"

"Yes," the man said suddenly. "I've got some family there. I'm
going to stay with them. I was in the marines—a Green Beret.
Saw a lot of action . . . I saw a lot."

Stu felt some of the tension unknot in his stomach. He realized
he'd been clutching the steering wheel too tightly and eased his
grip. At least the guy could talk if he wanted to. Maybe he was
warming up a little, thawing out. Whatever it was, Stu decided to
keep the mood light and the talk flowing.

As the miles flew on, the hitchhiker loosened up and talked of
Vietnam and the things he'd seen, of his difficulty in finding
work when he got home, of a year spent wandering around the
country and almost another year spent trying to get himself together and back into life. Denver seemed to offer a new hope, a
chance to start over.

Stu listened intently, asking questions, nodding in agreement.
He peered through the darkened windshield at the night—now
completely black and impenetrable—and at the two flat beams
that thrust from his headlights. Windswept fragments of snow
dipped into the light to disappear again on the other side. *Soon*

I'll be with my family, thought Stu. *I can get a good night's sleep and I'll be skiing in the morning.* "We'll be in Colorado soon," he said to his passenger. "We're almost to the state line."

The man made no comment. He seemed lost in himself again. "Do you ski?" asked Stu.

"Sure," the man answered, breathing heavily. "Hey, man, you know, I need to go to the bathroom. Could we stop?" He talked quickly and leaned forward in his seat.

"We're only about a mile from the interchange. I'm getting low on gas, so we'll need to stop at a gas station soon anyway." Stu kept driving. The light of the interchange came closer. The tall gas company signs rose up, glowing softly in the night.

"Couldn't we stop here?" the hitchhiker said, motioning to the side of the road. Stu shrugged and gave the wheel a quarter turn, easing off the gas as he did so. The Landcruiser rolled to a stop off the highway, several hundred feet from a dim circle of light cast by one of the giant poles which marked the interchange.

The ex-marine leaned on the door handle and stepped into the night. An icy blast hit Stu, and he tightened his jacket around him. Moments passed in silence. Stu waited. Then the hitchhiker clambered back to the car. He had one hand on the seat, the other held the door open. "Man, I think your right rear tire is awful low, maybe flat. You better check it."

The information came as a surprise to Stu; he'd noticed nothing unusual while driving. He shrugged and slid out of the car. It was dark and quiet on the road, not another soul around.

Stu stepped to the rear of the car and stooped over. He put his hand down to the tire; in the darkness he couldn't tell if it was low or not. Just then he felt a hot, piercing sensation in his side. *Ow!* He thought. *Pulled a nerve.* He straightened reflexively. Suddenly another burning pain struck him in the stomach. He whirled toward the hitchhiker.

Stu couldn't see the man standing next to him in the dark. But he felt a rush of air, of motion, then saw the glint of metal arching toward him. He ducked sideways and felt the skin of his eyelid give way and warmth flood into his eyes. *I've been stabbed!* he realized with a shock, throwing up his hands to cover his face.

This can't be happening to me, he thought. "Stop it!" he yelled. "Hey, stop!" The other man said nothing, his breath rushing through his teeth. Stu tensed. He felt another blow strike him on the shoulder. He tried to lift his arm, but it hung uselessly at his side. A wave of raw fear washed over him. *He means to kill me!*

"Take my car," he yelled. "Stop! Take my money. I'll give you anything!" Stu spun around, putting his hand out to stop the onslaught. He felt something hard. The knife. His hand closed around it. *If I can only get the knife.* But the knife was jerked away, cutting his fingers to the bone.

Stu lurched backward, but his attacker was on top of him, grabbing him and slamming the knife into his chest and stomach like a prize fighter punishing his opponent on the ropes. Stu loosed a cry of help into the cold air and fell to his knees.

Suddenly he was rolling. Over and over. The world spun; he could see nothing in the dark. He guessed he'd fallen down the steep incline of the interchange ditch. His heart was beating like it would burst. He decided to lie still. Maybe the attacker wouldn't follow him. *Stay down. Don't move.*

Then he heard a rush and felt the weight of the hitchhiker on his back. At the same time he felt a searing pain at the base of his neck as the knife sought the spinal cord. *I'm dead. This is it.*

Stu's only hope was to make the hitchhiker think he was already dead. So he lay still, offering no resistance.

It seemed to work. He felt the attacker move away, but he could hear the man breathing nearby. Stu knew the knife still hovered over him. He forced himself not to move, not to shiver.

For a long minute the man waited. Then Stu felt a hand grab his hair and pull his head up. Another hand moved to his throat. Quickly, expertly, the knife bit into his neck just below his right ear and traveled in a smooth arc to his left ear. His head was released and flopped back into the snow. *My throat's been cut. I'm dead.* His heart seemed to fly against his ribs. He lay still, straining in the dark for a sound, any sound, to tell him what might happen next. From somewhere high above him he thought he heard a car door slam—then nothing.

Stu's eyes were squeezed shut. He composed himself for death. "Lord, have mercy on me. I'm coming to you," he prayed. And a Bible verse came to mind. "Do not be anxious about anything, but . . . present your requests to God. And the peace of God, which transcends all understanding, will guard your hearts and your minds in Christ Jesus" (Philippians 4:6, 7). Immediately he felt the fear go out of him. Ready to die, Stu felt a peace descend over him and around him. Surprisingly he felt better. He decided to pray again. "God, forgive my sins."

A voice came to him, seeming to speak outloud. Stu heard the words plainly in the cold, quiet air. "Isn't there anything else you want?" it asked.

"Yes, help!" Stu blurted. Instantly his heart calmed. The voice was gone—had he heard it or not? He waited, thinking over what to do next. *Maybe I should try to get back to the road.*

Stu pushed himself to his knees and struggled to stand. He could no longer hold himself erect, but somehow crawled back up to the edge of the highway.

He stood and stumbled like a drunk toward the middle of the road. One lung had collapsed; he was out of breath and light-headed from loss of blood. *Maybe I can flag down somebody. Maybe they'll see me.* He stopped, leaning over to rest his hands on his knees, and for the first time noticed his clothes were covered with blood. Out of the corner of his eye he saw something move. He turned his head and saw the wheel and fender of a car. *Oh no! He's still here!* Stu thought. But in the same instant he heard someone close by saying, "What happened?" He saw a pair of boots and felt firm hands take him by the shoulders and half carry him to the waiting car. A state patrolman had seen him climb out of the ditch and had stopped to investigate.

The patrolman flung the door to the backseat open. "Get in," he commanded. Stu hesitated, "I'll get your car all bloody."

"You're bleeding to death. Get in!"

Stu felt himself bundled into the car and then heard the siren screaming into the night.

"We're ten miles from the nearest hospital. We'll be there in five minutes," the patrolman said. "Try to relax."

Remarkably, Stu *was* relaxed. His heart beat slowly, normally. As yet he felt no pain; his body was still in shock. His head was clear. Since praying, Stu had begun to feel more and more confident that everything would be all right. He lay back and closed his eyes, saving his strength for what was ahead and regretting that he was making a complete mess of the patrol car.

Moments later the vehicle jarred to a halt before the emergency entrance of a small hospital in Fort Morgan, Colorado. The patrolman had radioed ahead and the whole hospital had been placed on standby. Within minutes Stu's clothing was shredded off and his wounds explored quickly and expertly. The medical team worked furiously for three hours, unable to stop the worst of the bleeding. Stu watched calmly as doctors tested his vital signs and pumped new blood back into him.

"You won't make it here," a doctor told him. "We can't treat you; I'm sending for an ambulance to take you to Denver. They can handle it . . . if we can get you there in time."

Stu took the news as a matter of course. He nodded weakly. The doctor looked at him closely. "Do you understand what I've said? Do you know what this means?"

"Yes, I'm ready," he whispered, barely able to get enough air to speak.

The siren split the night. Stu cautiously peered around the driver to steal a glance at the speedometer. 105 mph . . . 110. It was snowing again, harder now. Stu lay back and tried to relax. The patrolman riding beside him, fearing Stu might enter Denver DOA, asked: "Could you answer a few questions? If we're going to catch that guy I need to know what happened."

They talked in low tones until Stu became too tired to respond.

Forty-five minutes later the ambulance barreled into the hospital's emergency entrance. Waiting attendants raced over with a gurney and pulled open the rear doors. Tugging gently on the restraining straps, they lifted a sheet over him. "To keep the chill off," one of them explained. Then they wheeled him through the emergency entrance into a crowd of curious onlookers. *They'll think I'm dead, with this sheet on my face,* Stu thought. He weakly raised an arm to pull the sheet away.

His parents, summoned to the hospital only minutes before, watched nervously from behind the orderlies. Stu's feeble movement reassured them.

As the doctors readied for emergency surgery, phone calls went out through the night to relatives, friends, people in his church back home. A twenty-four-hour prayer chain was organized. The police began systematically combing the area for Stu's car, tightening the net in the search for his attacker. The surgery was prolonged. Stu had been repeatedly stabbed in the chest as the attacker sought the heart. The doctors feared the worst. But as the chief surgeon worked, he found some hope. The heart had been spared, the spinal cord barely nicked. Perhaps even more remarkable, the long, ragged wound that sliced

Stu's throat from ear to ear had somehow missed the jugular, inflicting only minor damage.

As the surgery entered its second hour, police found Stu's car parked in front of a motel on the outskirts of the city. Inside a room they found the hitchhiker, wearing Stu's clothes. His own clothes, covered with blood, were found wadded up and stashed in the bathroom behind the toilet. They also found the knife—a small foldable hunting knife with a three-inch blade. When confronted, the man offered no resistance.

As Stu entered his third hour of surgery, doctors realized the full extent of his injuries. He had sustained twenty-seven separate wounds, many of them in the stomach and sides. He had been stabbed in the eye, the knife slicing through his upper and lower eyelid, but never touching the eye itself. His shoulder wound had damaged the thick muscle tissue, but would heal cleanly.

By the fifth hour of surgery, all of the wounds had been explored and treated, and the doctors began the long process of sewing them shut. They'd successfully stopped the bleeding—after nineteen pints of blood had run through him.

As the clock above the operating table crept into its seventh hour, the doctors put in the last of two hundred stitches they'd had to use to close Stu's wounds. He was then wheeled to the intensive care unit and the long vigil continued.

Throughout the hospital, word went out about the remarkable young man in ICU. A steady parade of people—many whom he'd never met—streamed to the hospital's chapel throughout the early morning hours to pray as Stu slept. His mother and father waited for an answer, a sign their son would be all right. The doctors weren't sure. They said they'd done all they could do but he'd lost so much blood. . . .

On the fourth day they moved Stu out of ICU and into a regular room. His progress was amazing. A miracle, the doctors said. Stu awakened from surgery hungry but clear-headed, able to talk quietly with his mother and father. "I'll be all right, Mom," he said. "Don't worry. I know I'll be all right." He was certain. Since his prayer in the ditch he'd felt a tremendous peace and reassurance. God was with him, he knew. Nothing would go wrong. He relaxed and viewed all the activity around him. Nurses checking vital signs; doctors prying beneath bandages, prodding wounds; orderlies and candy stripers poking their heads into his room just to see him. In a good-natured way, Stu chided the doctors and nurses for their lack of belief, talking openly about his prayers and the help from God he'd experienced. More than one person went away shaking his head in disbelief. It seemed impossible, but it was true.

, Merely two days after leaving the intensive care unit, Stu walked out of the hospital with a doctor's release. He felt good, rested and ready to get away from doctors and nurses for a while. But his doctor insisted he stay in Denver for a few weeks and check in every day.

"I was sore for weeks," Stu remembers. "I couldn't laugh, cough, or sit up. But I forced myself to be up and around, taking long, slow walks. I felt like an old man.

"Medically, there's no reason I'm alive today. I know that. I believe that if I hadn't trusted God completely, I would have bled to death in just a few minutes. But God's presence calmed me and gave me the confidence to face whatever lay ahead.

"I've had no bad feelings over my experience, no 'why me?' recriminations. People don't understand that. But then they don't know the tremendous peace that comes when God steps in to help.

"What purpose have I discovered for my experience? What dramatic life-changing revelations? Nothing like that at all. But I have come to appreciate Christ more, and all he endured dying for me on the cross. I've been close to death, and now I know I won't fear it again; God is there. He can take care of me, even in death."

Stu's attacker was quickly brought to justice in a trial that made headlines. The man was sentenced to long-term treatment in a mental hospital. Four weeks after his assault, Stu drove home— by himself—along the same road. This time he picked up no hitchhikers.

In my distress I called to the Lord.

Things don't always turn out so positively. Stu lived. Many do not. Because Stu lived, he can relay to us in horrifying detail the helplessness that comes with being attacked by someone without mercy . . . someone with death on his mind.

Stu lived, and seems to have survived without bitterness toward his attacker. Indeed, Stu has grown closer to Christ through his experience. He can assure us that the wounds from such an attack can heal—not only the physical wounds, but the psychological wounds of terror and bitterness can disappear.

Stu cried out to the Lord, and the Lord answered his prayer—amazingly, wonderfully, miraculously.

Make no mistake: God hates violence. He does not shrug off such attacks, and neither should we. After history's first murder, when Cain had killed his brother Abel, God said, "What have you done? Listen! Your brother's blood cries out to me from the ground" (Genesis 4:10). In that instance, God did not supernaturally intervene to stop the bloodshed. Nor did he save the victim, as he saved Stu. But he made it clear: The cry of the victim rings loud in his ears!

I recall words of Jesus which may seem odd to quote here: "Do not be afraid of those who kill the body but cannot kill the soul. Rather, be afraid of the one who can destroy both soul and body in hell" (Matthew 10:28).

How strong is evil? Strong enough to kill the body. But God is stronger. He is strong enough to prevent violence and often he does. He is strong enough to bring some good out of violence, as Stu would remind us. And our sense of justice demands this final note: God is strong enough to punish evil—strong enough to cast it into hell.

It was to this God that Stu cried out at the moment of his greatest fear. Lying in a snow-clogged ditch, punctured by knife wounds in every possible part of his body, his lifeblood leaking out, Stu turned to the Lord. He was heard, not because his prayers were unusually "faith-filled" at that moment. He was heard because God cares for those who suffer. And God not only hears, but he is strong and sure to answer.

We may struggle to comprehend why he does not always answer with deliverance. And yet we can see this much: It is prayer that connects us, in our times of greatest fear, to this God who is stronger than all evil.

It is truly, astonishingly amazing. The idea that I can voice my concerns out loud, under my breath, or in my mind; kneeling, standing, or running; thankful, confused, or angry; eloquently, casually, or incredulously.

And God hears.

"Help me," I say, and he does.

My best interests are his great concern.

Do I hear a vocal reply? "How are you this morning, God?" "Fine, thank you, Jim. And yourself?"

No.

When I talk to God do my feelings pulse with the energy of his presence? Not necessarily. When I snap out a request, does he hop to it with a prompt response? To the contrary, I am often kept waiting . . . and waiting . . . for the answer I want. And sometimes I get an answer I didn't want, at all.

The way God responds to my requests demolishes the idea that prayer is my good-luck charm and God the "Great Vending Machine in the Sky."

And yet, when I am most perplexed, when my confusion is thickest, when I am unclear where to turn or what to do next, I have this wild confidence that God knows, sees, understands, and cares. I am sure that if I talk to him, he will hear me and match my request, however inarticulate, with the precise response I would choose if my perception of things were not so limited and earthbound.

If he could hear Stu's cries in so desperate a situation as he found himself, he can surely take care of me.

In my distress . . . when my options are most limited, my resources most taxed, my confusion greatest—I will call on the Lord.

I am on a journey toward Honest Faith. Faith that can withstand a head-on encounter with tragedy—with sickness, death, violence. In the process of finding faith, I often stumble over my own distress, or feel acutely the despair of others. I could not find my way through my fears, frustrations, and questions—and toward God—without this landmark: prayer.

The cords of death entangled me; the torrents of destruction overwhelmed me. The cords of the grave coiled around me; the snares of death confronted me. In my distress I called to the Lord; I cried to my God for help. From his temple he heard

my voice; my cry came before him, into his ears.
    He reached down from on high and took hold of me; he drew me out of deep waters.
Psalm 18:4-6, 16

A PERSPECTIVE FOR DISASTER
EVEN CREATION GROANS IN PAIN.

Our present sufferings are not worth comparing with the glory that will be revealed in us. The creation waits in eager expectation for the sons of God to be revealed. For the creation was subjected to frustration, not by its own choice, but by the will of the one who subjected it, in hope that the creation itself will be liberated from its bondage to decay and brought into the glorious freedom of the children of God.

We know that the whole creation has been groaning as in the pains of childbirth right up to the present time. Not only so, but we ourselves, who have the firstfruits of the Spirit, groan inwardly as we wait eagerly for our adoption as sons, the redemption of our bodies. For in this hope we were saved. But hope that is seen is no hope at all. Who hopes for what he already has? But if we hope for what we do not yet have, we wait for it patiently.
Romans 8:18-25

THE NIGHT THE DAM BROKE

Most misfortune triggers the response, almost involuntarily, of blaming God. If God is all-powerful he ought to be able to avert a collision, or halt the advance of cancer, or prevent birth defects. But perhaps no calamity so tempts us to call God into question as does natural disaster. Violence we may blame on wicked people. Sickness and death we have come to expect as universal experiences, shadows we all pass through.

But natural disaster?

"Acts of God" seem so much within God's domain. With three simple words whispered to the winds, "Peace, be still," Christ spared his disciples when they were bobbing around Lake Galilee in a tiny wooden fishing boat during a life-threatening storm. Why won't he halt hurricanes or calm nervous earthquakes now? The lives at stake number more than twelve.

I remember driving through the tiny town of Meredith, Kansas, in the aftermath of a tornado. As we approached Meredith, we passed a thickly wooded area where gray metal roofing material had been twisted, pretzel-like, around tree trunks. And in town, the roof and upper story of a church had been carried away, while the piano sat amid the rubble apparently unscathed. But when I touched the keys, they would not play; their praise had been silenced.

I walked through a schoolyard and picked up a clock that had been blasted out of a classroom, its hands frozen on 2:10.

I was startled by the power of that storm, power I attributed to God. But if it *was* God's power, why couldn't he use it more constructively? And if it *wasn't* God's power, then where was he?

Those questions surfaced in the minds of many a few years ago when, as Christian students slept, mountains of broiling water spewed from a broken earthen dam high above the campus of their tiny Bible college.

In the wake of the storm, *Campus Life* editor Gregg Lewis slogged through mud and rubble to talk to the survivors.

Twice that night of November 5, the chief of the town's volunteer fire department drove his jeep up the steep, rain-washed gravel trail to check the water level and the dam of Kelly Barnes Lake, high on the mountain, hundreds of feet above Toccoa Falls in northern Georgia. The lake was swollen from four days of rain, and the creek runoff was heavier than normal. But when the rain finally slacked off around midnight, any danger seemed past.

However, deep below the surface, down inside the old dam, water began to seep through. A trickle became a tiny stream that grew and slowly ate away at the earthen base. At 1:30 A.M. on November 6, the lake broke through. The dam caved in with a *whoosh* and fifty-five acres of water, with a weight equivalent to seventy-five hundred freight train locomotives, careened down the mountain.

The narrow rocky gorge of the little creek funneled the entire mass of Kelly Barnes Lake into a raging torrent that snapped off trees and carried them downstream, toward the campus of Toccoa Falls Bible College. By the time it reached the 186-foot drop at the falls, just above the school, the 30-foot high avalanche of water was ripping down the mountain at 180 miles an hour.

Greg Bandy, a graduate student at the University of Georgia who was staying alone in his grandparents' house at the upper end of the campus, leaped out of bed when he heard the thundering crash plunge over the falls. "I looked out the window just in time to see a big transformer pole topple and explode like a giant flashbulb when it hit the water," he said. "In the eerie light I could see a wall of water as high as my second story window. I was sure the house was flooded." But as the water came gushing out of the creek gorge, it sloshed like water in a dishpan toward the other side of the valley, missing the Bandy house.

A second explosion ripped through the night as the water blew apart the steel and concrete roadway that spanned the creek, hurling chunks of broken bridge high into the air.

"I pulled on my clothes in a panic and raced downstairs. I grabbed a flashlight and ran all the way around the outside of the house. Trees and a car were floating in the yard. The house was on dry ground surrounded by water. But I didn't know how deep the water would get so I decided I had to get out. I plunged into the water and half ran, half swam through the dark backwater, away from the creek. When I finally reached the higher ground of the mountainside, I was trembling with fear and relief."

In their home just a few yards downstream from the Bandy residence, David and Barbara Eby had been lying in bed talking when a locomotive-like roar shook the house.

"The dam broke!" Barbara exclaimed as she leaped out of bed. But David didn't believe her until he joined her at the window and saw that rising water had completely surrounded the house.

Barbara rushed to the kids' room while Dave broke out a bedroom window to open a quick route of escape. As he worked, Barbara carried in seven-year-old Kim and went back for the two younger children. No sooner had she gathered them in her arms and stepped out of the children's room into the hall, than the first wall of water smashed into the house.

The fullest force of the water ripped through one wall of the kids' room and out the opposite side, flushing out the entire contents of the room with a 140-mile-an-hour torrent. Four things happened almost instantaneously: Barbara and the two youngest kids were swept down the hall and into the kitchen; David and Kim were washed into the living room at the opposite side of the house; the water level jumped almost to the ceiling; and the house twisted off its foundation and floated a short distance before the current pinned it against the mountainside.

Somehow David managed to find and hang on to Kim in the dark, water-filled living room. Together they climbed up a collapsed section of the roof to the top of the house. From there, when David could see the river's turbulence, he sensed the worst. He told Kim, "Mom, Kevin, and Kelley have gone to be with Jesus." Her matter-of-fact response, "I know that," calmed and reassured him.

For the next few minutes they huddled there on the roof, watching the water pull down the trees in their yard, hearing only the sharp snap of cracking trunks above the deafening roar.

The safety of the mountainside was only a few short feet away from their rooftop perch. David was sure he could toss Kim over to the bank, but it was rocky and he was afraid she'd be hurt. So he looked for another way.

From the edge of the roof he spotted a partition that had fallen from the house against the bank—that looked like the best route to safety. So he grabbed Kim and together they jumped down to the makeshift bridge. But the partition broke, dumping them into the water where David lost hold of Kim.

Sucked under the house by the churning water, David knew he was going to die. For one terrified moment he thought, *No one even knows where I am.* Then he realized, *God does.* That's when the water banged him against the house. He grabbed for a hold and slowly pulled himself out and up against the undertow. The instant his head broke the surface and he gulped in his first breath, two little hands clasped his neck and he heard Kim laugh and say, "Daddy, don't let go of me again."

Once more his daughter's words and spirit encouraged him. Fighting for handholds, David pulled himself and Kim along the house toward the kitchen's screen door. And he began hollering, straining to outshout the water as it thundered past. "Barbara! Barbara!"

Even as he yelled, he thought, *Why bother? I know they're gone.* But he kept calling, "Barbara! Barbara!"

Incredibly, he heard a voice calling back, "Dave! I've got Kevin, Dave!"

"I've got Kim," he answered.

When she called, "I've got Kelley," he couldn't believe all five in the family were OK. It was too overwhelming to be true.

David finally pulled himself and Kim to the door just a few feet from where the rest of the family clung to a pole that ran from a kitchen counter to the ceiling.

"Dave," Barb gasped, "I'm getting so tired. I don't know if I can hold on much longer." But she did hold on. The water level began to drop and twenty minutes later, when it was finally safe, the Eby family waded to shore.

Across Toccoa Creek from the Eby house, the residents of Forrest Hall, the boy's dorm, had spent a typical Saturday night. Chuck Dowell, who roomed in the dorm's walk-in basement, had turned off his light and dropped right to sleep a little after midnight. A rumbling sound stirred him but he didn't awaken until a giant wave crashed in through his window.

"I don't know how I got out," Chuck said. "The door was closed when the water hit and I don't remember opening it. All I know is that I was swimming in chest-deep water one second and the next instant I found myself in the stairwell walking up."

At the end of the hall, Kenny Carroll had been sleeping until he heard what he thought was a noise in the hall. When he saw a sheet of water spreading across his floor he reached for the door at the head of his bed and opened it. A sudden gush of water yanked the door out of his hand. By the time he jumped to his feet the water in the room was a foot deep.

When he rushed into the hall, Kenny could feel the force of the water. "I remember thinking, *If I slip, I'll drown*," he said. So he ran—in the wrong direction—toward the middle of the hall. He'd only gone a few steps in the darkness before he bumped into the two guys coming out of the next door. "By this time," he said, "the water was above our knees, so we joined hands and worked our way back along the wall toward the stairs. When we got to the stairwell the three of us had to force the door open against waist-deep water. The entire stairwell was full by the time we reached the first floor. The whole thing had taken only five or ten seconds. We ran all the way to the second floor before we stopped at a window just long enough to see the water blast right through the music building next to the dorm."

By then the upper halls of the darkened dorm were a madhouse of shouting. "The dorm's flooding—everybody get out!" "We're all going to die!" "Flood! Everybody run!" "There goes my car!" "Hurry! Get out of here before the dorm goes!" "Eby's house is floating away!"

"I yelled for clothes because I was wet and freezing," said Kenny. "Someone threw me a pair of pants and somebody else pulled me into a room and handed me a shirt." Within minutes everyone in the upper floors emptied out of the dorm. But three of Kenny's and Chuck's friends never escaped the basement.

Within seconds of the time it crashed over the falls, the front wall of the flood had slammed through the dorm and was charging down the creek valley, ramming through the streamside homes like an angry bulldozer, plowing their splintered remains into a tidal wave of red, muddy water and rubble. That broiling wall of water and debris rolled on downstream toward a cluster of mobile homes the students of Toccoa Falls Bible College called Lower Trailerville.

When Bob Harner was awakened by shouting and looked out his trailer window, a foot of water already covered the ground. Thinking this was a flash flood similar to one a year earlier, Bob yanked on his clothes and called for Tiap, his wife, to get their two-year-old son, Robbie, so they could wade to higher ground.

But by the time they got to their back door a few seconds later, the trailer had lifted off its blocks. Bob helped his family climb onto the roof of the neighbor's car that floated against the trailer door. A wave slammed over them, knocking Bob off one side of the car and washing Tiap, with Robbie in her arms, off the other.

That first wave was followed by a higher mass of water, trees, cars, and chewed-up debris. This second giant wave lined up trailers like a train and sent them shooting down across the open pasture below Trailerville.

For a short distance, Bob rode the flood like a body surfer, fighting to keep himself flat on the surface. "But when my head rammed into a logjam of debris, my body dropped perpendicular and the current yanked me under and tumbled me along the bottom.

"Nails, glass, and stone slashed the soles of my feet as I shoved off the bottom trying futilely to find the surface. Three times the water dragged me back down before I could breathe any air. But as I tried to dive to the bottom for another try at pushing off, I sensed a bright light. In that instant I saw my concept of God. I can't explain it and I wouldn't want to try, but I felt a brightness and a glory there with me in the water. Suddenly, it was as if a hand reached down and jerked me right up. One second my lungs were bursting and I was trying to dive to the bottom to push off and the next second I popped to the top like a cork and took a relaxed, normal breath.

"I thought I saw my wife sweep by holding onto a tree limb, but I wasn't sure and I couldn't reach her. I grabbed onto a car that floated me out of the current's mainstream. Then I swam twenty yards or so to a floating jam of debris. I crawled across that for another fifty to sixty yards, falling into the water and clambering out again several times before I reached shore.

"It wasn't until I crawled out onto shore that I really thought about my son," Bob said. "I knew he didn't make it. But the verse came to me, 'Let the little children come to me, and do not hinder them, the kingdom of heaven belongs to such as these.' "

By the time Bob Harner dragged himself onto dry ground, the debris piling up under a bridge downstream had dammed up the floodwaters and transformed the pasture and the flats that had been Lower Trailerville into a twenty-foot-deep lake.

Bob found he was one of four people washed up on a small hill at the end of the pasture. During the following few minutes, he waded back in and out of the water dragging more survivors to shore until fourteen people in all huddled on the hill in the chilling autumn darkness. Bob gave his shirt to one of the women. And together the group prayed.

As the shattered remains of their homes and possessions floated by, this little bank of battered survivors turned to God to thank him for his protection. But the relief they shared at being alive couldn't dispel the common fear that family or friends had been lost.

A couple of bright spots broke the long, dark wait for rescue workers to come and carry out the seriously injured members of the group. When one woman who had lost her husband and all three children in the flood led the group in reciting the Twenty-third Psalm, a feeling of trust descended on that flood-besieged hilltop. "I think we all felt God's calming presence," Bob said.

"The other high point concerned Archie Smith," he went on. "When we pulled Arch out of the water he thought his whole family had drowned. But as we waited, we called word around the bank about who was with us. Someone hollered back, 'Hey, Archie. Your wife and kids are safe in Upper Trailerville.' As tears of relieved joy splashed down Archie's face, we all praised and thanked God together."

Others wondered about their own families. Were they safe or had the flood wiped out their lives? It would be hours before Bob Harner learned for sure that his wife and son had died. Yet there in the midst of personal darkness and despair, Bob and the other survivors were able to share another man's joy.

Two hours later, when the rescue teams finally reached them, Bob Harner and the rest of the group walked out together. For them, the danger was over. The giant lake that had formed in seconds was slowly shrinking and flowing away.

Meanwhile, back upstream where the creek had returned to its banks, Greg Bandy found the Ebys on the mountainside where he and they had fled to safety. The family huddled against the cold, wrapped in soggy sheets and window curtains they'd salvaged from their home. So together they waded back through the muddy quagmire of the Bandy yard and into the dry house for a fresh supply of clean clothes.

As the college's dean of men, David Eby worried about the students on campus. So he and Greg found a fallen tree over the creek and crawled across.

"When we got to the campus we finally realized how serious things were," Greg said. "I heard several people were missing, so I thought I'd help look. I slopped through the mud behind the boys' dorm, stopping at each window and shining my flashlight into each mud-caked room. At the fourth window, I had this feeling someone was in there. So I flicked the light around, searching the corners until I saw it—under a mattress a hand stuck up out of the muck as steam rose around it.

"That's when everything hit. I went into semi-shock and felt very sick. I'd had big plans of helping search for bodies of victims, but that one quick glimpse was enough. I recrossed the creek, went up to my room and did something I hadn't done much of for months. I got out my Bible and read and prayed. I could just imagine God saying, 'Why are you coming to me now—what about all the other times?' And I couldn't sleep."

Fortunately, Forrest Hall had been the only occupied campus building in the flood's path. But no cleanup could begin and no assessment of damage could be made in the nightmarish darkness. So most of the school's students sat through the night in darkened LeTourneau Hall. They grouped in small circles around candles and flashlights. Scattered voices quoted Scripture promises, others called on God's help. From time to time soft singing broke out.

As the night progressed, messengers began shuttling news

back from the hospital and from Trailerville. As each death list
and survivor report was read aloud, friends and acquaintances
wept in sorrow or relief. Then they prayed and waited restlessly
for the next word and for morning. But no one was prepared for
the shocking devastation revealed by the gray morning light. The
deep valley below the campus had been completely gutted. Giant
trees were uprooted. The houses and the trailers were gone.
Only scattered clues of splintered wood, chunks of walls and
roof, muddied clothes, shattered toys, and broken bodies strewn
down the muddy red valley hinted at the life that had been there
just hours before.

Morning also brought an onslaught of newsmen, cameras, and
world attention. Within hours, money, supplies, and other tokens
of sympathy and concern began to pour in. The residents of
nearby Toccoa opened themselves and their homes to the town
and students of Toccoa Falls. The days of grief and emptiness
that followed were punctuated by a string of funerals and
memorial services. The college closed for a week for initial
recovery. And the survivors started the slow, painful process of
cleaning up and rebuilding their lives.

In the emotional vacuum of a disaster's aftermath, the "why"
questions begin to loom larger than life and death.

Some Christians have a stock answer for any tragedy: "It must
have been God's will." But what does that mean? Does God reach
down to poke holes in dams?

Other Christians look for natural explanations: Men build
dams that weaken with age. And the natural laws God built into
this universe as part of his plan keep working—like the law of
hydraulic pressure that forces water through a weakened dam and
the law of gravity that pulls thousands of tons of water down a
mountain at devastating speed.

But that doesn't answer all of the questions. Why does God al-
low disasters? Why doesn't he rescind his natural laws to pre-
serve people—especially Christians—from such tragedies?

I expected to find these questions being asked by the Toccoa
Falls survivors. The newsmen had asked them these questions,
and surely they'd asked themselves and God. They had to question the capriciousness of the flood. One entire family survived
by floating to safety on a hide-a-bed when another trailer crashed

through theirs. Rescue workers pried open another crumpled trailer to find a husband and wife safe in each other's arms; the spot where they were standing was the only part of their trailer that had remained intact. Why did these people live while thirty-nine others died?

There's never a shortage of opinion on the "why" questions. Newsmen can summarize the disaster stories for the end-of-the-year review, theologians can postulate their hypotheses, and the barroom philosophers in all the north Georgia taverns and cafés can debate their own views every Saturday night for years. But not even the people closest to disaster, the survivors themselves, can arrive at satisfactory conclusions. Dave Eby admitted, "Even my children want to know why God let us live and let so many of their friends die. And I've spent hours talking to other survivors who can't understand why they survived when the others didn't; they almost feel guilty about it. When you think about thirty-nine people dying—all people you know—you have to wonder why. But I don't know that we'll ever know—there's just no simple answer."

By the time I visited Toccoa Falls, the survivors I talked to had pushed the "why" questions to the back of their minds. Instead of struggling for explanations, they were reflecting on lessons they had learned, focusing on results instead of cause.

"One night the week after the flood, I stood by the creek and looked upstream toward the falls," Greg Bandy remembered. "The creek gorge was aimed like a gun at my house. I was struck by the awesomeness of what had happened. I should have been hit and drowned by that first wall of water.

"Right then I began to appreciate life as a gift. I had to face the fact that before the flood, while I had been a Christian, I hadn't been living the way I knew God wanted or expected. The flood made me realize the importance of living each day for God. And my level of relationship with him has deepened in the past months because of that."

Every Toccoa Falls student I asked, even those who sat out the flood in the safety of a dry campus building, said one of the most important things they had gained from the flood was "a new appreciation for life."

People who lost their homes and other possessions told me they had learned to trust God more than ever before to provide them with the material things they need. In some cases he used the generosity of concerned, loving people to provide survivors with better clothes, cars, and other things than they had before the flood.

But it was the victims who faced death themselves, and whose families perished in the flood, who evidenced the strongest faith in God and his dependability. Instead of bitterness and despair, they spoke with conviction about their confidence and trust in God.

"Thoughts of my wife and son keep popping up," admitted one student who lost his wife and baby son. "Those memories hurt so much I have to rely on God's strength. I couldn't have made it without his help."

"I'd placed my family's life in God's hand a long time before the flood," said Bob Harner. "Now that Tiap and Robbie are in his hands, I still have to trust him.

"I know the Lord gave me incredible strength the week after the flood. I stood by my wife's and son's caskets as four hundred people filed by. Many of them were weeping and God gave me the strength to comfort and encourage them.

"I'm not saying I didn't have grief or didn't cry. I did. And some days still seem painfully empty. Thanksgiving and Christmas were especially tough. So was our wedding anniversary. But I've learned that God will give me the strength and peace when I need it most. And each day gets a little easier."

I went to Toccoa Falls wondering how these Christians' faith held up in disaster. For two days I listened as people whose voices still cracked with emotion spoke of their unshaken trust in God and his care. I heard stories that sent chills up my spine and brought tears to my eyes. But I left, inspired by the survivors' rock-solid belief, convinced that the Toccoa Falls flood hadn't destroyed faith, but strengthened it.

The fresh growth of spring covers many of the scars. The rubble has been cleared. Life in the little valley town goes on like it always did. But if you visit Toccoa Falls today and talk to students and townspeople, you too will find an inspiring confidence in God—a faith tempered by tragedy.

As one survivor explained, "We know that God was with us through the flood. He was with those of us who escaped. And he was with the thirty-nine people who died. Because of the flood we know that God will be with us through anything we ever have to face."

Even creation groans in pain.

You can hear it in the churning of a twister. You can feel it in the shudder of a tremor. You can see it in the raging turbulence of a flash flood. Creation groans.

Sun beats down on cracked soil as drought extends famine and hunger and death. And creation groans.

Cancer cells spread unchecked through the body, choking first health — then life. And creation groans.

Hailstones hammer at a jetliner's steel skin; one engine fails and then another. Powerless, the man-made albatross tumbles to earth — life is lost. And creation groans.

God created a lush, productive, weed-free garden. A place of health and life. But mankind turned away and disease and death, thorn and thistle disrupted God's good provision of nature.

Jesus once told the story of good seed falling onto good and bad soil. Then growing. Or dying. It strikes me that, were it not for our spiritual insurrection, the story would have made no sense. "What is Good News?" we would have asked. "I have never heard *bad* news. And," we would have continued, "what is this stuff called 'bad soil'— rocky, thorny, weedy? I know only good soil. Productive. Life-giving."

To know where "bad soil" came from, you must start in Eden. There, man rebelled — and a process was set in motion. In Eden's lush undergrowth weeds and thorns extended their shoots. In time, thunderclouds formed and twisters' snake-shaped funnels fell to the ground. Earthquakes rumbled. Hurricanes howled. Man's rebellion was felt even in the miniature cellular world. Bacteria and virus raged, sapping health from the life of the planet's people.

We live in an abnormal world. It bears marks of the greatness that once was Eden, but it also harbors disease and death, drought and disaster.

Things on the planet today are not how God intended them. Not, we might even say, the way nature itself would like them to be. Nature groans. It writhes in its agony, not unlike a patient struggling with cancer's painful spread.

We may safely conclude that cyclones and tremors, tornadoes and flash floods do not come so much from the hand of God as they do from the fingertips of evil. Man's (and Satan's) early waywardness has flung the whole creation into a restrained chaos. I say "restrained" because I believe God has maintained a check on the self-destructive bent of mankind and his domain. Things might well be worse.

The question remains though, and tugs at us: "Why doesn't God intervene?" We might temporarily dismiss the question by saying simply, "He has not chosen to."

But that's not quite true. According to Scripture, he *will* intervene. In the future. He will crush insurrection and set nature itself straight. There will be an end to suffering and sickness and tears and death.

If we are to take the New Testament at its word, the question is not, "Does Christ have the power to intervene?" It is not even, "Will he intervene?" It is more a question of timing: *"When* will God intervene?"

The answer: We do not know.

And here the matter is complicated by our differing perceptions of time. To us, bound in a cycle of suffering and death and by limitations of time and space, every day is like a thousand years. What's holding him back?

If the New Testatment is to be accepted, the delay is somehow bound up with our option to choose. God is not through giving people the option of turning to him, and therefore he's not finished with the present, flawed world order. He's simply not ready to reverse the curse that our waywardness has set in motion. He's not ready to crush evil — and punish those who are evil. So, until God steps in to change all this, even his people are not fully sheltered from what this fallen world has become.

Creation groans in pain. And in hope. Hope of better things that are certain to come. We groan, too, anticipating the creation of a world without the pain and hardship that plague our days now.

In the meantime, God is committed to bringing good out of even our most tangled experiences. He tells us, and urges us to believe, that over the long haul the suffering will ultimately seem brief and light compared to the coming glory.

Believing that, or not believing that, we ache with antici-
pation.

> *Our present sufferings are not worth comparing with the glory
> that will be revealed in us. The creation waits in eager expec-
> tation for the sons of God to be revealed. For the creation was
> subjected to frustration, not by its own choice, but by the will
> of the one who subjected it, in hope that the creation itself will
> be liberated from its bondage to decay and brought into the
> glorious freedom of the children of God.*
>
> *We know that the whole creation has been groaning as in
> the pains of childbirth right up to the present time. Not only
> so, but we ourselves, who have the firstfruits of the Spirit,
> groan inwardly as we wait eagerly for our adoption as sons,
> the redemption of our bodies. For in this hope we were saved.
> But hope that is seen is no hope at all. Who hopes for what he
> already has? But if we hope for what we do not yet have, we
> wait for it patiently.*
> Romans 8:18-25

> *Who shall separate us from the love of Christ? Shall trouble
> or hardship or persecution or famine or nakedness or danger
> or sword? As it is written: "For your sake we face death all the
> day long; we are considered as sheep to be slaughtered." No,
> in all these things we are more than conquerors through him
> who loved us. For I am convinced that neither death nor life,
> neither angels nor demons, neither the present nor the future,
> nor any powers, neither height nor depth, nor anything else in
> all creation, will be able to separate us from the love of God
> that is in Christ Jesus our Lord.*
> Romans 8:35-39

LOOKING TO THE END — A LONG, BRIEF LIFE
WHAT IS YOUR LIFE? YOU ARE A MIST.

Now listen, you who say, "Today or tomorrow we will go to this or that city, spend a year there, carry on business and make money." Why, you do not even know what will happen tomorrow. What is your life? You are a mist that appears for a little while and then vanishes. Instead, you ought to say, "If it is the Lord's will, we will live and do this or that." As it is, you boast and brag. All such boasting is evil. Anyone, then, who knows the good he ought to do and doesn't do it, sins.
James 4:13-17

A BURDEN AND A PLEASURE

It had been a gradual process, her deterioration. The time came when she and Grandpa could no longer care for their old two-story home. They moved to a small apartment and the old house and its store of memories stood empty. Still and silent. After Grandpa's death, Grandma deteriorated quickly. She moved again. She needed help getting around and remembering things.

I recall visiting her and feeling certain she was winging it. Inside she was really thinking, *Who is this kid? And what's he doing in my living room?*

Finally, she died.

In those, my earlier years, old age seemed to be just that: old. Life dragged on for a long time. The body slowed, but plodded on. And on. Until the years rolled to a stop and death at last came.

I am far from old, but my opinion has changed. Life is not long. It is short. And if the elderly are sometimes quite ready to die, and feel like life has been forever, it is, I think, more from fatigue than the sense that life has been truly lengthy.

As the elderly freely discuss all the change they have witnessed, we can get a wrong idea of time. My grandmother, for instance, used to tell me of standing at her back porch as horse-drawn wagons moved westward along the rise a mile away. Over the years, she told me, the wagons became cars and the busyness increased. Captivated by such tales, I thought, *She's ancient!*

As all this personal history is recited to the young, who have seen so little change, it gives the impression that much time has passed, that life itself is long. In truth, it's not so much that life has been long but that change has been swift.

I have often wondered how our perception of life would shift if we were to grasp the brevity of life early, while it yet seems so long. How would it alter our values? How would life, for us, change?

In the following, and final, story, Evelyn Bence captures something of the shortness of life by showing us the final moments, and the burden and pleasure of the old.

I glance around the room to make sure no one is looking . . . and quickly touch my grandmother's still, cold hand. Just two days before, I had held its warmth for hours as she lay in her hospital bed. Then her hand had been all black and blue from the doctor's many unsuccessful probes to place a needle into her vein. Now both hands, folded neatly in her lap, are white and motionless.

A few months before, as I was helping her to slowly climb the stairs, she told me, "I've lived eighty-seven years, and that's too long. I'm just too old to be anything but a burden. Don't ever wish that you'll be old like me." Then she looked at me in a way she had many times before — as if she were envying my twenty young years and trying to forget the lifetime that lay between us. She started to cry, quietly and helplessly. I longed to be able to give her the steady legs, clear sight, and limitless energy the years had worn away. But all I could do was kiss her cheek and tell her that I loved her.

After Grandpa died suddenly two years ago, Grandma wasn't able to live alone in their big house. So, her children decided she should rotate between my aunt's house and ours. She resented giving up the independence she and Grandpa had been so proud of.

But once she was alone, Grandma was forced to let her children care for her. Grandpa's strength had been her strength; without him she was physically, childishly weak. Mentally, Grandma was still strong enough to hate the thought of her middle-aged daughters caring for her as she had once cared for them. But while that was half her mind, the other half knew she had no choice. Both she and her children knew she could not go to a rest home. Only castaways went there. So, the decision was final. That's when she moved in with us.

She didn't bring a lot with her. Her favorite dresses, one for each day of the week, and a few personal items—her Bible, a box of writing paper and cards, some old photographs and letters, and a musty cigar box full of, of all things, buttons. My mom tried to convince her to leave the buttons, but she wouldn't hear of it. "No, I need them," was her short reply.

She set that old cigar box on her bureau. Every Monday she checked all her dresses to see that no buttons had been lost. Then she checked her box to be sure it was still full.

Caring for her was like caring for a five-year-old. When we went out, we got a sitter. And Mom cooked special meals for Grandma because she had diabetes. Dad gave her insulin shots every morning when he was home, but he traveled a lot and Mom was afraid to do it. So when Dad was away, a neighbor who was a nurse came in every morning. Of course, Grandma insisted on paying her daily. The nurse refused at first, until she realized Grandma's pride was more important than the money. So she learned to accept it with a pleasant smile.

Smiling—that was something else. Everyone had to force an extra ounce of sweetness into his personality because Grandma became offended at the slightest harsh word. One evening Dad was particularly aggravated with Mom. He'd disagreed with her when Grandma was out of the room so Grandma didn't know any details. But she could feel tension in the air at dinnertime. She was sure my dad was mad at her instead of Mother. After dinner, as she was drinking her coffee, she mustered up all her courage and broke the icy silence. "Paul," she said to Dad, "I wish you'd tell me what it is that I've done that's made you angry with me." The sentence ended between muffled sobs.

We all stared at her, shocked that she was taking the tense feelings personally. Dad explained, as best he could, that he was not angry with her. But she silently shuffled off to her room and closed the door on her tears.

She spent most of every day sitting in her favorite rocker. Right after breakfast she'd read her large-print Bible out loud, whether anyone was listening or not. The rest of the day she sat at the large picture window staring out across the valley and up to the hills on the other side of the river. She seemed to draw strength from the quietness of the countryside.

She talked a lot about "being a burden" and Mom would always say something about "not a burden but a pleasure." Then Mom'd tell Grandma how grateful she was for all Grandma and Grandpa had done for her. Grandma would smile and nod her head, being temporarily assured of her continued welcome.

Last week she was too weak to get out of bed and she blacked out for a few minutes several times a day. We took her to the hospital on Wednesday. After a lot of testing the doctor told my mom that everything had worn out. He didn't tell Grandma anything, but she knew. She started talking about her funeral. She wanted my uncle who was a minister to give the message, my brother and sister to sing "Amazing Grace," and she wanted to wear her blue dress.

Friday she told me that she didn't want anyone to pray that she'd live. She just wanted to die quickly. I decided I shouldn't pray for her to die, but maybe I could just not pray for her at all.

Sunday I went back to visit her. She was much worse and I didn't think my mom should stay alone, so I ended up staying all day. One of us held her hand constantly to give her comfort and to keep her from jerking her arm and pulling out the needles. We listened to her barely audible whispers, which were sometimes coherent, sometimes not. When she was coherent, she always talked about the same things—dying and saying good-bye. She kept thanking Mom for her patience and apologizing for all the inconvenience she'd caused.

I was only there fifteen minutes before I started to pray for her—that she would die. I prayed for her off and on all day.

Now there are smooth red rosebuds pinned to her blue dress. Her chest is still and her eyes closed. My parents' friends have called and said they are sorry, but wasn't it nice that she'd had such a full, long life. My parents answer yes, we're fortunate to have had her with us this long.

But at breakfast this morning, Mom finally admitted something to me: "Grandma was a burden, as well as a pleasure."

What is your life? You are a mist.

If Evelyn's grandma—or yours—could write these last few paragraphs, what would she say? Looking back over a long, brief life, would she focus on the hard times, the sorrows, the injustice? Would she stress the limitations that held her back, the sicknesses that hounded her, the grief she endured as friends and family died? Would she single out encounters with suicidal friends or with violence or disaster? Would she tell us the worst that happened was her own death as it overtook her?

As she surveyed her life in retrospect, would the good times be so overshadowed with life's depressing challenges that she would say, "Life is just not worth the hassle, don't bother with it"? Looking back, would she see life as a panorama of goodness, joy, and beauty, or evil, sorrow, and ugliness?

The question is important. We are wondering about faith and tragedy. We are acknowledging that life is littered with tragedy, much of it almost unbearably painful. In view of that, we voice the question, "Is life any good at all?" Then we add the postscript, "And does faith make a difference?"

I visualize Evelyn's grandmother at death stepping from time to timelessness and being caught up in a world of unimaginable perfection. A realm that is all this world was originally intended to be, plus much more.

She is caught up in splendor, and is, I believe, fully satisfied. She knows hardship and death are forever behind her, not before her. Any nagging questions have been resolved.

And so, if we were to ask her to compose these final paragraphs, to summarize her earth-life, to compare suffering here with satisfaction there, we might expect we'd read her words and feel all the more depressed. Why stay here? What good is life?

But I don't think that's what she'd say. I think she'd say there is no point in trying to compare existence here with life there. She might characterize heaven as glory, earth as comparative gloom. But I think she would say more.

I think she would tell us not to resent life for the hardships it tosses at us. She'd tell us that what may seem unendurably long now will soon seem to have been brief, and that the suffering we endure here has greater value than we can imagine.

I think she would tell us with awe how much we are loved by God—more than we could dare to dream. She would tell us how he, the great God, feels our pain, walks with us through our hurting, shelters us from much that would destroy us. She would point us to the common things—shelter, food, water—as the often-forgotten evidence of his care.

She would probably tell even more. She would not bad-mouth this life. She would speak of how its goodness, joy, and beauty foreshadow heaven itself. She might point to the expanse of space or the intricacy of the microscopic world. She might point to giant redwoods, craggy canyon walls, a sunset over the Pacific, the face of a friend. I think she would remind us of the wonder of human love, and would point to the good that one person may do for another. She would urge us to see the hand of God in *this* life, not just the next. She would tell us he is vast and great, but close and tender.

If Evelyn's grandmother—or yours—could write these final paragraphs, I think there's one more thing she would stress, perhaps ahead of the rest. I believe she would tell us that even though we cannot adequately *compare* this life with the next, we should not think of them as two unconnected realities; on the contrary, they are intimately and intricately related. This goes beyond God "over there" seeing things and hearing things "over here." She would tell us that this life is linked directly to that life. That today is a prelude to the ultimate tomorrow. Or, she might say, they are both parts of the same song.

Decisions we make here, now, affect our existence there, then. She would tell us, with sternness and determination, of judgment before God in *that* life for how we handled the gift of *this* life. And she would remind us that we can stand before him guilt-free because of Christ.

Because of Christ. If Evelyn's grandmother—or yours—were writing these final paragraphs, she would remind us of the hardship and brutal execution Christ endured for us on this planet, in this life, so that even in our deepest hardships we could find faith in him.

Faith in him, even in the face of tragedy.

And so I have reflected on certain landmarks along this journey toward that Honest Faith. And this landmark is in some ways the most important: *What is your life? You are a mist.* If I mistake this life for being longer or more permanent than it really is, I might postpone the journey itself. I might settle down in comfort and forget faith altogether. Instead, I am faced with the shortness of my life, even when it *feels* most permanent.

What is life really?

Merely a mist.

I understand mist. Like an early-morning fog that clings to the ground, but dissipates under the warmth of the rising sun. Like steam from a teakettle on the boil. Or the faint cloud that swirls toward the kitchen ceiling when you lift the lid off the peas. Like a jet's vapor trail drifting across the late afternoon sky. It's here, then gone. Brief.

Everything in me yearns for permanence. But instead I roll into life like morning fog, then vanish under the rising sun of death. I'm here, then gone. Life is brief.

It doesn't seem that way at the time. Today has a deceptively forever feeling. I don't feel death closing in on me. Life, mine anyway, feels like it will simply roll on endlessly.

In his epistle, James says, "Don't be dogmatic about your week's agenda. Don't say: 'Tomorrow, I'm going to town.' Do say: 'If the Lord wills. . . .' " But this seems odd. If I know today what I plan tomorrow, why preface it with a salute to God's will?

Why?

To remind me of my faulty perceptions of time and forever.

Why?

To nurture in my mind a view that life, however long, however brief, is to lived under the direction of God and his ways.

Why?

Because the mist that is my breath is a moment-by-moment gift from God.

If I live to a ripe-old age, experience the fullness of good life, and at last, exhausted, close my eyes in a death of natural causes, even then life will have been painfully brief. But I have no guarantee that it will be so long.

Only that it will be worth living.

Now listen, you who say, "Today or tomorrow we will go to this or that city, spend a year there, carry on business and make money." Why, you do not even know what will happen tomorrow. What is your life? You are a mist that appears for a

little while and then vanishes. Instead, you ought to say, "If it is the Lord's will, we will live and do this or that." As it is, you boast and brag. All such boasting is evil. Anyone, then, who knows the good he ought to do and doesn't do it, sins.
James 4:13-17

LAST WORDS

I began this project realizing that it might become an exercise in inducing depression. In the short space between these covers we have peered into the experiences of death and disaster, sickness and suicide, handicaps, aging, and violence. Experiences we would expect to be remote, and yet which we find knocking on the doors of our lives. Or a friend's.

We might be tempted to conclude that happiness is the exception in life, not the rule.

We might conclude that God is impotent, ignorant, or cruel. He flicks his fingers and jets tumble from the skies. He arranges terrifying rendezvouses between oppressors and innocent bystanders. He fans the flames of diseases that burn through our bodies.

We might be tempted to draw such ghastly conclusions except that we've found a document, the Bible, that puts these hardships into perspective, that gives us clues to the puzzles of life, and that introduces us to a strong and caring God who walks with us through the most hellish circumstances.

And though the Bible may stop short of dispensing answers to banish our questions and dispel our doubts, it does give insight. Clues. Landmarks to help us find our way through the journey of faith.

And what are these landmarks, but hints about the meaning of our hurt? Suggestions about how God uses the most hideous of our encounters—how he salvages them—for some mysterious good.

Consider them once more:

LANDMARK ONE: *When I am weak, I am strong* (2 Corinthians 12:9, 10). He helps us face our limitations, our handicaps. He turns our weakest moments into displays of his great strength in us.

LANDMARK TWO: *Suffering produces perseverance* (Romans 5:3-5). He offers help in sickness. He uses our suffering—our hardships—to perfect our character, to produce in us patience, experience, hope in him.

LANDMARK THREE: *Outwardly we are wasting away, yet inwardly we are being renewed* (2 Corinthians 4:16-18). He enables us to confront death. He gives us such a view of eternity that we can see the pain of time through the grid of a glory-filled forever. He shows us that though we may deteriorate outwardly, though the body shell crumbles, inwardly we experience ever more vital health.

LANDMARK FOUR: *We comfort others with the comfort we have received from God* (2 Corinthians 1:3-7). Even in suicide's aftermath, God comforts us. He teaches us to look for and find his comfort, coming to us through our relationship with him and through our interaction with other people enduring similar painful experiences. He teaches us the easing of our own pain that comes as we reach out to comfort others who hurt.

LANDMARK FIVE: *In my distress I called to the Lord* (Psalm 18:4-6, 16). In the midst of violence, God gives the assurance that he hears our prayers and is ready to stretch out a hand to help us, to comfort us. He lets us know that he hurts with us.

LANDMARK SIX: *Even creation groans in pain* (Romans 8:18-25). God gives us a perspective for disaster. He helps us understand something of the extent of the hell that our wrong choice has unleashed even on the creation. But he shows us too a glimpse of hope. The hell that exists now will change and fall into place, subservient to his better ideas. He gives us a sense of his timing. And though it is painful to await that resolution, we at least sense some purpose and wisdom in the painful delay.

LANDMARK SEVEN: *What is your life? You are a mist* (James 4:13-17). Through the insight God gives, we can make sense out of aging. Our bodies grow old all too quickly. Our days, though they seem long, are few. We are preparing for something better during this long, brief life. Knowing its brevity, we ought to carefully reevaluate our priorities.

There's much we don't know. Many mysteries remain unresolved. But God has given us enough insight to keep us trusting him with an Honest Faith, to keep us running toward him—at times, perhaps, crawling toward him—even if it is only with why-shaped questions on our lips.